# How to Go to Therapy

# CARL SHERMAN

# HOW TO GO TO THERAPY

*Making the Most of Professional Help*

NEW YORK

Copyright © 2001 by Carl Sherman

All rights reserved under International and Pan-American Copyright Conventions. Published in the United States by Random House, Inc., New York, and simultaneously in Canada by Random House of Canada Limited, Toronto.

AtRandom.com Books and colophon are registered trademarks of Random House, Inc.

Library of Congress Cataloging-in-Publication Data

Sherman, Carl.
How to go to therapy: making the most of professional help/Carl Sherman.
p.   cm.
Includes bibliographical references and index.
ISBN 0-8129-9187-7 (pbk.)—ISBN 0-679-64723-6 (e-book)
1. Psychotherapy.   I. Title.
RC480.5 .S475 2001
616.89'14—dc21    2001041281

Website address: www.atrandom.com

Printed in the United States of America on acid-free paper

24689753

*First Edition*

# *Preface*

There's something anachronistic about psychotherapy. Resolving your problems by *talking about them,* week after week, seems quaintly nineteenth-century in a world of high-speed Internet access and high-tech medicine. To cure our ills, we have pills. (Distrust chemicals? Opt for herbs.) Or buy a videotape to learn how to live without fear, or lighten your dismal moods, or overcome your addictions.

As a journalist, I have been writing about mental health for nearly two decades, for psychiatrists and for the general public. At times I wondered whether psychotherapy would long outlive the twentieth century. The cover of one national magazine featured a glowing green-and-yellow capsule and pronounced Prozac a wonder drug; a few years later, another depicted the bearded progenitor of psychoanalysis and asked, "Is Freud Dead?"

In the professional conferences I covered in the 1980s and '90s, the talk turned increasingly from personality to neurochemistry, from the mind to the brain. And to money. While science was pushing the envelope of neural knowledge, the American health insurance industry was putting on the brakes. The same shifts in policy that sent us home from the hospital "quicker and sicker" after surgery balked at paying for treatment that took months, if not years. From an accountant's perspective, all those fifty-minute hours didn't add up.

But in the year 2001 psychotherapy is still with us—robust, by all indications, as it ever was. It's increasingly clear that therapy works:

people do better with it than without it. Evidence from carefully designed studies has in fact found certain kinds of therapy as effective
as drugs in taming anxiety and depression. Even the new neuro-
science offers surprising validation: state-of-the-art scanning instru-
ments suggest that successful psychotherapy can help the brain
function more normally—much the way medication does.

One consequence of therapy's vitality is its diversity. If you are
looking for professional help, you're likely to encounter a bewilder-
ing array of philosophies and methods, each with its own dedicated
proponents. You'll also find that guides through the forest are in
short supply. Those who practice psychodynamic therapy, or cognitive therapy, or client-centered therapy have seen their method work
and may, understandably, find it difficult to be unbiased about the
field as a whole.

This book is an attempt to fill that gap. It was written not by a
psychotherapist but from the perspective of a professional observer
(and occasional consumer) of mental health care. I've tried to look
closely, write objectively, explain clearly, and give you the information most useful in finding the help you need: details about qualifications and credentials, as well as brief accounts of the ideas behind
the different kinds of therapy, how they work, what actually happens
in sessions, and what science has to say about their effectiveness.
And lots of resources to investigate on your own.

Several themes stand out. Therapy is an individual matter. You
may want to relieve very specific symptoms, like fear of flying, or to
feel generally better; to achieve practical goals (improve your ability to concentrate or get along with others), or highly personal ones,
like growth and self-exploration. No one size fits all.

But beyond the diversity, all good therapy has something in common: a validation of basic human values. Therapy isn't something
that's done to you, but something you do for yourself in collaboration with another person. Most of us seek help at a time of uncertainty, when self-confidence is low. At its best the experience
confirms our own capacities—and affirms the power of honesty,
courage, and serious effort.

The theories, concepts, and techniques that characterize different approaches are fascinating and important. But in the last analysis, most research comes up with a surprisingly simple conclusion: at the center of successful psychotherapy is a human relationship, informed by intelligence and heart. This represents something that has always been precious, perhaps never more so than today. May the pages that follow help you find it.

# Contents

*How to Go to Therapy*

# Chapter 1

—

# DO YOU NEED THERAPY?

Things aren't going well. You leave for work with a sense of dread and come home half-dead with fatigue. You fight incessantly with those you love—or can't find anyone to love. The toll of smoking or excessive drinking is obvious, even to you, but you keep on doing it.

Maybe something happened to knock you off balance. You lost your job a month ago, and now it's hard to get up and get dressed. A friend is terminally ill, and you can't put thoughts of him out of your mind. Since that emergency landing at O'Hare, every business trip gives you nightmares.

Or there's nothing really wrong, nothing you can put a finger on. But one day you realize that you've been struggling through the motions in a miasma of low-level discomfort and dissatisfaction. Whatever you do doesn't seem like the right thing, and none of it gives much pleasure.

What are you going to do? There's no shortage of books to tell you how to heal whatever ails you, no lack of talk-show gurus with wise advice on everything from beating the blues to finding lasting love or the job of your dreams. Maybe you've assembled your own little arsenal of strategies that help when the burdens get heavy and the skies refuse to brighten: taking a long, strenuous walk, a hot bath, a vacation. Volunteering at a soup kitchen. Cultivating your garden.

Friends and family are an age-old source of solace in times of trouble. Human beings are essentially social creatures; we need each other, and a sympathetic ear, an encouraging word can work wonders. It's been shown that simply having a confidant—someone you can trust to listen and care—reduces stress, eases anxiety, and lifts mood.

But sometimes the usual fixes just don't work; you know you've got a problem, and it's not about to go away. And the question comes up, *moves* up rapidly from the back of your mind (or perhaps it's suggested—diplomatically or otherwise—by a friend or loved one): should you go for therapy?

## What Is Psychotherapy?

We all know what therapy is—until we try to pin it down, and realize how many very different things have come to carry the label. "Therapy" can last six weeks or six years. It may involve two people—you and the therapist—or your whole family, or even a group of strangers. You may talk about today's crisis or last night's dreams, or events you can scarcely remember. You may be encouraged to keep a diary of your thoughts, or to free-associate. To pound pillows or to take pills.

What do they all have in common? No matter what particular form therapy takes, the essence is an ongoing relationship. Researchers who seek to find what makes therapy successful return again and again to that central fact: whatever else happens, the closeness and trust between patient and therapist—what is called the "therapeutic alliance"—is a key factor. It even appears to be important when medication is the main treatment.

Therapy is a unique type of relationship, and what makes it valuable is what sets it apart from friendships, working partnerships, family connections, and love affairs. Its purpose is well defined: understanding and change. It comes into being, that is, to help you identify and understand dysfunctional ways of thinking, feeling, and acting, and to generate more productive and satisfying ways of thinking, feeling, and acting.

Friends and family members want to help us when we're in distress, and the advice they offer (with or without solicitation) can be useful. But the kind of counsel you'll get from a therapist is different. Rather than being simply instructive ("Here's what you ought to do"), it's likely intended to be a catalyst, to quicken your own ability to work things out.

Perhaps the most essential difference between therapy and other significant relationships is a matter of balance. You and the therapist are collaborating on a single project: helping you deal with your problems and achieve the changes you want. There is no other agenda.

This makes it very different from even close, supportive friendships in which you pour out your troubles and get a sympathetic ear and even useful feedback. Eventually, your friend will get bored, or tired, or simply need to talk herself. The essence of friendship is mutuality: you meet each other's needs. In therapy, your needs are what matter. The word itself, *therapy,* comes from a Greek word meaning "to serve." You receive the service—of being listened to, understood, helped—not out of friendship, love, or altruism, but for a fee. Crass as it sounds, this is a strength of therapy—there are no strings attached.

Another essential quality of therapy is *safety.* If it works well, you can be yourself, say what you feel, reveal your fantasies, fears, and aspirations, without repercussions. The therapist's professional role includes receiving your disclosures without moral judgment or rancor. You won't be ridiculed, censured, or resented—not when you speak, not a week or a year later. Can your best friend, spouse, or parent offer this guarantee?

You can say whatever you need to and know it will go no further. *Confidentiality* is a key component of the therapeutic relationship, as it is in certain religious settings. With the exception of well-defined circumstances (to be discussed fully later), the therapist is bound by ethics, and by law, to reveal nothing that transpires during your sessions. The communication, in fact, is *privileged,* which means that the therapist cannot be required (again, with exceptions) to reveal what you've said, except under court order.

Part of the safety zone in which therapy takes place is its reliability. It generally happens at the same place and at the same time, and follows a predictable format. It isn't contingent on your performance—the therapist won't get up and leave if you fail to keep her entertained or to live up to her expectations. Even intimate relationships can be jeopardized when one of the partners goes through personal changes ("You don't seem like yourself"), but in therapy, change is the whole point.

In addition to everything else, therapy is an *educational* experience. Some therapists actually describe what happens as a kind of learning, and compare their role to that of a teacher or coach. But even when this isn't explicit, any kind of effective therapy leads you to step back and reconsider what you may have always taken for granted, to try out new ways of looking at yourself, your emotions, and your world.

## Who Needs Therapy?

There's little doubt that many people could use professional help. Nearly a half-century ago, when epidemiology in this area was somewhat less rigorous than it is today, one study found that 81.5 percent of the population of Manhattan had "signs and symptoms of mental distress."

Using more precise definitions, the 1999 U.S. surgeon general's mental health report suggested that in the course of a year 22 to 23 percent of Americans have a diagnosable mental disorder—that's 44 million troubled people. Most suffer from some form of depression or anxiety severe enough to cause marked distress or interfere with work or personal life. A 1993 study by the National Advisory Mental Health Council found that nearly one American in ten experienced *significant* functional impairment due to emotional ills—their problems made it truly difficult to go about their daily lives.

"Just as practically no one gets through life without a physical ailment, very few can without significant psychological ailments, conflicts, and stresses," says Jeffrey Binder, Ph.D., director of doctoral and master's clinical training at the Georgia School of Professional Psychology in Atlanta.

An identifiable crisis, loss (of a job, romantic partner, or close relative), or trauma propels many people into therapy. For others it's the culmination of a lengthy process; the problem is long-standing, and now the time seems right. Symptoms, like anxiety or difficulty concentrating, have become severe enough to interfere with your life. Perhaps your work is suffering.

"The key idea is perception," says Sharon Hymer, Ph.D., a clinical psychologist practicing in New York City. A family conflict may have been simmering for years, or a romantic disappointment may be just the latest act of a long-running drama. But on top of that, there's a feeling of *demoralization.* "People go to therapy when they perceive themselves in a crisis that they can't resolve by themselves and with the help of friends." (The kindling of hope, experts say, is often the first big benefit of effective therapy.)

Feeling you are out of your depth is a key indicator that it's "time to ask for some help," advises the American Psychological Association. Think of therapy when you feel trapped, with nowhere to turn, when it seems that things aren't getting better, when worry becomes chronic and never leads to any answers, or when emotional unease spills over and affects the way you eat or sleep, or takes a toll on your job or personal life.

Psychiatrists often treat those at the more seriously ill end of the spectrum. The American Psychiatric Association lists marked personality change, extreme highs and lows, excessive anxiety, anger, hostility, or violent behavior as indications for a prompt consultation. Thoughts (or talk) of suicide are a warning that *immediate* help is needed.

The mind and body are closely connected, and some signs that therapy may be helpful are physical. Unexplained, often vague symptoms—fatigue, frequent headaches, backaches, or other troublesome pains, frequent digestive upset, even pesky skin conditions—can reflect depression, anxiety, or a burnout level of stress. Such problems may accompany emotional distress or take their place. When a thorough medical work-up finds nothing, consider a psychological explanation.

On the other hand, a life-threatening illness such as cancer or heart attack, or a painful chronic condition like arthritis, often outstrips one's ability to cope. Psychotherapy doesn't take the place of medical care, but it can supplement it: in fact, substantial data suggests that people with serious illness do better physically if they take effective steps to deal with the emotional turmoil it creates.

While there's little solid data on just who seeks therapy and why, a widely cited 1995 survey by *Consumer Reports* found that nearly half of four thousand readers who went for professional help were "in considerable pain." Besides mental disorders like anxiety and depression in their various forms, the motivating forces included family or sexual problems, work woes, stress-related symptoms, problems coping with grief, and difficulties with alcohol or drugs.

Most significant emotional problems, however, remain untreated. The surgeon general's report noted that only one third of people with a diagnosable condition were getting any sort of help with it, and just over half of these were in treatment with a specialist such as a psychologist or psychiatrist. You may be in serious distress; you've done what you can to make things better, and it hasn't been enough. Your work, family life, or friendships are somewhat the worse for wear. Yet you hold back. You just can't take the next step toward getting help.

Why does this happen so often? For one thing, there's a persistent notion that we *should* be able to do it on our own, that it's shameful to need help. Some people fear that they'll give up control of their lives by submitting to the influence of someone with a sophisticated knowledge of human nature, or coerced into taking drugs. Or that they'll be "homogenized" by therapy, lose their individuality, become some sort of processed clone. They think that therapy must be a lengthy process that inevitably requires rehashing all of childhood and opening up a Pandora's box of repressed impulses. Or that nothing will really help—their problems are so hopeless that they are beyond therapy.

And there's stigma. Although much progress has been made in recent years, a lot of baggage still attaches to mental health problems— the idea that anyone who seeks therapy is "crazy" or "disturbed," somehow damaged or less than whole.

Many such attitudes come from images of therapy and therapists promoted in our culture. We laugh at endless analysis à la Woody Allen and set box office records to see movies featuring a Hannibal Lecter–type psychiatrist who is as expertly manipulative as he is malevolent. (Some psychiatrists have described the Lecter portrayal in *The Silence of the Lambs* as "devastating to the profession," and expressed concern that such images may prevent potential patients from getting the help they need.)

The best way past these obstacles is information. Learning, for example, that an explicit goal of good therapy is to help you become *more* individual and creative, not less so. That many effective kinds of therapy focus on the present and pay little attention to ancient history. That the "nothing will help" feeling is itself a symptom of emotional trouble (specifically, depression), not a realistic appraisal.

One last barrier to seeking therapy is simply not knowing how. What do you do to find a therapist? How can you ensure that he is competent, qualified . . . right for you? Is there reason to believe his approach is likely to be helpful? The aim of this book is to assist you in this quest.

## Chapter 2

—

# WHO CAN HELP?

*Choosing a Therapist*

When you visit a physician, you know what she is—the "M.D." after her name may not tell you everything about her intelligence, experience, or areas of expertise. But you can assume she's had the training and passed the tests that, by consensus and law, qualify her to treat your bodily ills, and indicate that she is legally and ethically obligated to follow a well-established code of conduct.

But when you seek mental health care, you find people who call themselves psychotherapists, psychologists, social workers, nurses, and counselors, among other things. It's a jumble out there—a jumble of names, titles, and degrees. Before you start looking into more complex questions of how "good" a therapist is, you need to know *what* she is. Keep in mind, however, that a title or degree will tell you so much, but no more.

A *psychotherapist* is someone who is in business to do psychotherapy. It's purely a descriptive term; as a title it means nothing. Anyone can list himself as a "psychotherapist" in the Yellow Pages, hang out a shingle, or run a magazine ad, just as anyone can call himself a philosopher or healer. He needn't have a license and is accountable to no state board or professional association for his actions. He has not agreed to adhere to any code of ethics or principles.

This is not to say that an unlicensed psychotherapist cannot be well trained, brilliant, and highly scrupulous. But then again, he may be a scoundrel, or a criminal (a psychiatrist or psychologist who has lost his license for unethical behavior can still practice as a psychotherapist). *From the title itself, you have no way of knowing.* And if things go wrong—he violates your trust, uses unorthodox methods that cause great harm, or disappears in the middle of your crisis, you may have virtually no recourse.

A *psychiatrist* is a licensed physician. She has gone to medical school and received the same basic training as your internist, and presumably knows a few things about the human body and the various things that go wrong with it. She followed her medical training with four years of psychiatric residency—courses and practical experience devoted to the study and treatment of mental illness.

Psychiatrists are the only mental health professionals allowed by law to prescribe medications. Their training should also give them special insight into the complex connections between medical and emotional illnesses. But the title does *not* necessarily indicate competence in psychotherapy. Residency training programs differ widely in the amount of time they devote to this area, and some pay it little attention. (This is changing: as of 2001, psychiatric residency programs are required by the Accreditation Council for Graduate Medical Education to have their trainees demonstrate competency in basic types of psychotherapy.)

In the essentials of therapy—establishing an effective relationship with patients, and helping them achieve insight into their problems and work toward the changes they desire—a psychiatrist may be expert, or woefully inadequate.

A *clinical psychologist* also needs a license to use this title. He has advanced training—the minimum varies from state to state but generally includes a graduate degree and at least two years of supervised clinical experience. Most psychologists have doctorate degrees (Ph.D., Ed.D., or Psy.D.), although in many states those with master's degrees can be licensed as well.

A psychologist's training generally includes the study of theories of behavior and an acquaintance with research methods. His grounding and experience in one or more types of psychotherapy may be thorough, or fairly minimal. When you go to a licensed psychologist, however, you do know that he can be held accountable for his professional actions.

Note: Someone with a Ph.D. who calls himself a psychotherapist is not necessarily a psychologist. The degree may reflect training in an unrelated field.

A *clinical social worker* is also a licensed mental health professional. Some social workers practice in a hospital setting and have little to do with therapy. Those who work directly with patients as therapists generally have the designation A.C.S.W. (certified social worker) or L.C.S.W. (licensed clinical social worker), for which they typically need two years of supervised experience after a master's degree and must pass a state examination.

While a social worker's psychotherapy training may be similar to a psychologist's, it is likely to put extra emphasis on a "systems" view of mental health, which pays more attention to the social forces impacting the individual, and on his relations with family, community, and other groups.

*Marriage and family therapists* are licensed in most states, but not all. A license generally means a master's degree, two years of supervised clinical work, and a state exam. These professionals specialize in treating couples and families, but may work with individuals as well. Members of the American Association for Marriage and Family Therapy have met training and education requirements and agree to abide by the organization's code of ethics.

Many family therapists are also certified or licensed as clinical psychologists or social workers. A psychologist who has a special interest in this area, for example, may undergo additional training and supervision after his initial certification.

A *psychiatric nurse* has a nursing license and should have additional training in psychotherapy. But there is no specific degree or credential that guarantees this. Most work in hospital settings, but some do individual therapy in outpatient clinics. In some circumstances, psychiatric nurses can prescribe medication under the supervision of a physician.

*Counselor* is a loose term that generally refers to professionals, often but not always with a master's degree, who treat specific problems like substance abuse, stress disorders, or short-term crises, rather than more serious persistent disorders. Any clergyperson can do *pastoral counseling,* which may use the techniques and approaches of psychotherapy in a religious context, or consist of basically spiritual advice.

Most states have licensing for counselors. Those who hold licenses (including pastoral counselors) generally have similar training to social workers: at least sixty hours of graduate credits and two years of supervised clinical experience. Membership in organizations like the American Association of Pastoral Counselors or the American Counseling Association suggests a degree of expertise.

## Naming Names

As the foregoing should have made clear, it can be useful and even important to know a prospective therapist's title, but that's only the beginning. That Dr. X is a licensed psychologist or psychiatrist tells you nothing about her empathy, intelligence, or skill, or for that matter what kind of therapy she practices.

Nor will it tell you how helpful to you she is likely to be. Research has confirmed what common sense suggests: not all therapists—even those with comparable training—are alike in their effectiveness. "The therapist matters" was the conclusion (in fact, the title) of a paper that examined results in seven different clinical trials using several kinds of psychotherapy. Although the patients were assigned randomly, and the therapists were following a manual to make sure they applied the same kind of therapy, some clearly got better results than others. In one study the patients of one therapist showed a nearly two-thirds reduction in symptoms, while another's actually worsened.

Three of the therapists took part in more than one therapy trial, and their effectiveness appeared consistent: those who excelled with one group of patients also did well with others.

You can open the Yellow Pages, find a psychologist whose name you like and whose office is convenient, make an appointment, and check him out. But most people who have had experience in therapy advocate a more conscientious approach.

As with a physician (or, for that matter, an automobile mechanic), a recommendation from someone whose judgment you trust is the best place to start. If that person is professionally knowledgeable about the field, so much the better. It's unwise if not unethical for a therapist to treat someone she knows socially, but that doesn't mean she can't refer you to a colleague.

Your family physician or internist can very likely suggest a therapist. But often such referrals are made on the basis of relatively shallow professional networking. The doctor believes the therapist is reputable and presumably has heard no complaints about him, but may know little about his personal qualities, training, or how he handles therapy. What's more, many physicians will treat emotional problems themselves, and while you may receive competent care this way, results have been found to be somewhat less compelling than with a mental health professional.

Friends who have been pleased with their therapists are often willing, even eager, to send others their way. In this case, take the opportunity to get more details. What does your friend like and not like about her? What is her style—is she extremely laid-back, or does she actively ask questions and make suggestions? What goes on in a typical session? Does your friend leave sessions feeling better or worse?

Sharing a therapist can be a delicate situation. If you or your friend feel uncomfortable with such an arrangement, a reasonable alternative is asking your friend's therapist to refer you to a colleague.

*Professional associations* supply names of their members. If you want to see a clinical psychologist, the American Psychological Association [www.apa.org; 800-964-2000] will direct you to one of its local branches, each of which operates a referral service for members who pay to be listed. Although the amount of detail supplied about individual psychologists varies from state to state, listings may include education, training, areas of expertise, and the forms of therapy they do.

Membership in the APA doesn't necessarily imply that a psychologist has more training or education than is needed to be licensed, but the APA has a formal, quite detailed code of ethics, which members are bound to follow or face disciplinary action.

The American Psychiatric Association [www.psych.org] will also refer you to practicing members; call the local district branch (find it at the national organization's website, or call the national headquarters of the organization at 888-357-7924).

The American Association for Marriage and Family Therapy [www.aamft.org] maintains a "therapist locator" service, which lists more than fifteen thousand members, with details on education, training, and professional affiliations for some.

*Consumer groups* maintain lists of therapists. Check the National Mental Health Association [www.nmha.org; 800-433-5959] for names and numbers of community mental health centers, hospital clinics, and the like.

NMHA does not refer to individual therapists but directs callers to the Psychotherapist Referral Network (800-THERAPIST). When you call this private company, a licensed mental health professional will take information about your problem and preferences and match you with a licensed therapist in your area. The service is free to the public, but therapists pay a fee to be listed (and have submitted documentation of their degrees, professional memberships, and areas of advanced training).

Your local Mental Health Association branch (find it at the NMHA website or in your telephone directory) may offer other referral information.

Groups and foundations organized to help people with specific disorders may also direct you to therapists with appropriate experience and skill.

*Hospitals, medical centers, and medical schools* often operate outpatient clinics (usually with a sliding fee scale) and will also refer to affiliated therapists in the community.

A *community mental health center* is an option if cost is an issue. Such facilities are chronically underfunded, so there may be a wait of days to weeks. You can find a CMHC through your state or local mental health or health department.

*Managed care and health maintenance organizations* keep lists of participating professionals, and you may be limited to these if you want your insurance to pay for your therapy. (This is a knotty issue, and will be discussed at length in Chapter 13.)

## Choosing a Therapist

Before seeing or even calling a prospective therapist, you may save unnecessary effort by finding out something about her. The *Dictionary of Medical Specialists* lists psychiatrists, along with details of education, training, hospital connections, and professional affiliations. It is available at most public and university libraries.

Note: Only *board-certified* psychiatrists are listed. Those who are board-eligible—they have been trained as psychiatrists but haven't gone through the formal process to be certified as specialists by the American Board of Psychiatry and Neurology—are not.

Background information on more than fifteen thousand clinical psychologists is available in the *National Register of Health Service Providers in Psychology* [www.nationalregister.com]. For social workers, consult the *Registry of Social Workers*.

If you simply want to assure yourself that a therapist is licensed (e.g., as a psychologist or social worker), contact your state's attorney general's office to find which licensing authority to call. A list of state agencies that license psychologists is also available at Psychwatch.com, a website for mental health professionals [www.psychwatch.com/license.htm].

When you call a therapist for an initial appointment, take the opportunity to determine some formal details, such as fees, managed care participation, and availability (e.g., can you see him in the evening?), as well as degrees and professional affiliations.

But there's no substitute for a face-to-face meeting. Whatever the particular method, the success of therapy appears to depend on a working relationship, and in this regard, intangible factors of "chemistry" may be more important than such formal criteria as professional memberships and specifics of training.

Do you have the sense you can work together? Some people have strong feelings that their therapist should be male (or female), gay (or heterosexual), of a certain age, of the same religion or ethnic background as themselves, or otherwise "like them" in key ways. Research has associated similarity in such areas with more effective therapy, although it may be less important than other factors and makes little difference to most patients. It's a personal matter; such characteristics cannot be dismissed as trivial, in any case, if they make you more comfortable with your therapist and feel better understood.

In your first session, you'll spend most of the time talking about yourself—what brings you there, what you hope to accomplish in therapy. Often a good therapist will make observations, raise questions, and foster a constructive dialogue from this first meeting. He may describe (or you can ask about) his approach to therapy, what happens in a typical session, his experience dealing with your particular problem. Respect the therapist as a professional, but don't discount your feelings: in your gut, does his approach sound feasible?

Flexibility is desirable in a therapist. It used to be that just about all psychologists were dead set against the use of drugs, and psychiatrists invariably advocated them, but that is changing, as mental health professionals have come to recognize that no one approach is best for all. Whether or not he can prescribe, look for an open mind about medication.

Empathy is as essential in a therapist as in a good friend; the ability to see the world from your point of view fosters the closeness and trust that make therapy more likely to work. Most effective therapists convey a positive attitude about people in general, about their work, and about themselves—unsurprising when you consider that the first thing therapy must do is rekindle the hope that problems can be resolved and life can get better.

The authoritative *Harvard Guide to Psychiatry* suggests that the first moments of meeting can provide telltale indications of a respectful and helpful attitude: a handshake, perhaps, and a welcoming, courteous demeanor. A relaxed, comfortable posture, neither intrusively close nor aloof, rather than a tense concentration on gathering data bodes well for the future.

It's important to feel that you're not only listened to empathically but also understood. A good therapist should be able to communicate in words a real comprehension of what you're going through. Something rings true when he reflects on what may be leading you to have distress.

You may leave the first session with a positive feeling of trust, and confidence that therapy with this person will be profitable. Or you may feel that the two of you are poorly matched. But don't be surprised if you feel uncertain: any relationship may take a little while to get off the ground. If time and finances permit, a trial run of two or three sessions before you make a decision is worth the trouble.

Lester Luborsky, Ph.D., professor of psychology in psychiatry at the University of Pennsylvania and one of the foremost researchers in the field, advises interviewing several therapists and choosing "the one you feel offers the best potential for a positive working alliance." This, admittedly, has its drawbacks: most therapists expect to be paid for their time, even in an exploratory interview; on a more personal level, you may be reluctant to elaborate on your problems before a stranger, not once but several times.

In any case, there should be limits to therapist shopping. Looking for Dr. Right can be a substitute for the commitment and work that effective therapy requires—just as endless searching for the ideal relationship keeps some people from ever achieving a satisfactory one. If you feel understood and in the hands of a competent professional, try to forget the fact that there are thousands of other therapists out there, one of whom may be even better.

# Chapter 3

—

# WHAT CAN YOU EXPECT?

*The Rules of Therapy*

Beginning therapy is likely to make you feel nervous and uncertain. It's a new enterprise and a new relationship, taking place on unfamiliar ground. What should you expect? What conditions can you assume, and what must be negotiated? There are some ground rules that all therapy follows—or should follow—and some elements that may vary from one situation to another. The clearer you are about both, the more confidently you can proceed.

Licensed therapists of all kinds are bound to follow ethical guidelines—to behave, that is, in a manner that their profession, by consensus, has concluded will provide the essential basis of safe, effective therapy. Infractions may lead to consequences ranging from censure by their professional organization to loss of their license to practice.

With very few exceptions, nothing inappropriate that a therapist does that is otherwise legal is subject to criminal prosecution—even a very incompetent therapist is not likely to go to jail for his misdemeanors. Any licensed therapist, however—psychologist, psychiatrist, social worker, or counselor—can be sued for malpractice, on the basis that his professional actions caused harm to the patient *and departed from accepted standards of care.*

In other words, a licensed therapist has a good deal of reason, beyond her professional pride and personal values, to adhere to certain basic rules in her work and to exercise respect and restraint in the conduct of therapy. As a patient, you have the right to expect to be treated in a fair and predictable way.

This includes the right to information: according to the *Principles for the Provision of Mental Health and Substance Abuse Treatment: A Bill of Rights,* a consensus statement endorsed by all the major professional therapist groups, a prospective therapist must be forthcoming about her training, education, and experience. In the role of patient, it's easy to be intimidated by the therapist's aura of authority. But your rights include having your questions about the effectiveness of the treatment she recommends, and about possible alternatives, taken seriously and answered honestly.

Psychologists should "provide only those services and use only those techniques for which they are qualified by education, training, or experience," according to the American Psychological Association's *Ethical Principles of Psychologists and Code of Conduct.* The ethical standards of psychiatrists and social workers similarly specify therapists' obligation to work within the limits of their competence. If situations arise during therapy that they aren't qualified to treat, they should be willing to bring in another professional for a consultation or refer you to someone who can help. They should not continue providing services beyond the point where it's useful to you, nor should they abandon you without making provisions for your continued care.

Central to the ethical and legal principles that guide therapy is the fact that it is a *fiduciary* relationship—one in which you *entrust* yourself to a professional's care. As when you enlist the services of a doctor, lawyer, or banker, your needs must be paramount, and his gratifications limited to an appropriate fee (as well as professional satisfaction in a job well done and, perhaps, humane delight in helping others). In no way should he exploit the situation for any other gain.

To make sure that your needs are served without compromise, and to preserve the sense of safety that allows therapy to be effective, your sessions should take place within *boundaries* that set it off from the rest of your life.

**Separate lives.** Ideally, your therapist is not someone you deal with socially, professionally, or in a business capacity. Although ethical guidelines (such as those of the American Psychological Association) recognize that in settings like small towns or academic communities a certain amount of outside-therapy contact is unavoidable, they stress the therapist's responsibility to avoid arrangements that may undermine therapy or cause harm to a patient. Generally, therapists stay out of your life—they won't attend your wedding or join you in business ventures. (There are exceptions: in certain kinds of behavior therapy, for example, a therapist may accompany a patient in confronting situations that arouse anxiety.)

While gifts (from you to the therapist, never vice versa) are a gray area—most see little harm in a token, such as a small office decoration or a souvenir from a trip—anything substantial is to be avoided. Bartering (goods or services in exchange for therapy) raises the possibility of exploitation and is a poor idea.

**No sex.** The ethical codes (of psychiatrists, psychologists, and social workers) forbid sexual intimacy of any sort with any patient, as well as therapy with former lovers. The ban extends into the future as well; the American Psychological Association's code of ethics allows for sexual intimacies with a former patient two years after termination of therapy but only under "the most unusual circumstances"; while psychiatrists and social workers are required, by their respective ethical codes, to refrain from it altogether.

The rationale for such strictures isn't hard to understand when you consider the highly personal nature of therapy. Alone with your therapist repeatedly, perhaps revealing thoughts and emotions that you otherwise keep hidden, relying on the intelligence and judgment of a professional, you may experience sexual feelings that have more to do with the situation than the persons involved. Therapists are human too; particularly if their personal lives are troubled or unsatisfying, they may feel drawn to an attractive, vulnerable person they see at such close quarters.

A crucial element of the therapist's professional role is the ability to recognize these feelings and to refrain from acting on them—even if a patient brings them up or acts in a provocative, seductive, or entirely willing manner, and even if the signs of true love seem unmistakable to both parties. If sexual contact were not banned even after therapy is over, the mere possibility could contaminate and undermine the whole process.

Sex with a patient has led to a number of lawsuits in recent years, including some that generated a great deal of lurid publicity. It has cost some offending therapists their licenses, and in more than a few states (including Minnesota, Wisconsin, Georgia, and California) it is a violation of criminal law that can result in imprisonment. In most of them, "consent" is not a defense, in recognition of the fact that the nature of the relationship makes it impossible for the patient to freely give or withhold consent.

**Confidentiality.** Another critical element of the boundary that keeps therapy safe and sacrosanct is your full confidence that what you say in a session will go no further.

While privacy is an essential right whenever you seek medical care, it is absolutely central to psychotherapy. Without confidentiality, the trust and openness that make therapy work are inconceivable; you can't say what you want to and need to if you fear it may come to the attention of others.

Therapists are expected to expend considerable effort in maintaining the confidentiality of what transpires in the therapy room. Even when consulting with colleagues or discussing scientific issues, psychologists are called upon by their code of ethics to avoid details that could identify the patient. They are bound to exercise care in keeping and disposing of their records. Without your permission, your therapist should not even indicate to a third party that you are in therapy.

Group therapy is a more complex situation. While the therapist is under the same obligations of confidentiality as in individual therapy, members of the group are not professionals and don't have a code of ethics to uphold. Generally, all agree not to reveal details of what happens, but you should realize that this is guaranteed by nothing stronger than each individual's conscience and sense of honor.

There are exemptions from the therapist's vow of silence. Under law, she must inform authorities if a patient represents a danger to others or to himself; if a third party is threatened, the therapist may be required to alert him directly as well. Therapists (like teachers, physicians, and other professionals) are obligated to report their suspicions that a child or other vulnerable person is being subjected to abuse.

When disclosure of otherwise confidential information is required or allowed, it should be kept to the minimum necessary for the purpose (for example, to collect a bill for services, a therapist may reveal how long a person has been treated but shouldn't elaborate about his fantasies). If you institute a lawsuit against a therapist, you may have to waive much of your right to confidentiality.

The obligation of confidentiality doesn't run both ways. It's your therapy, and you are, for the most part, free to talk about it (a right that has left a visible mark on contemporary memoirs and talk shows). You also can consent to have records of your therapy made available for various purposes, as part of screening for a sensitive job, for example, or, most commonly, for health insurance claims.

In fact, if you want to have therapy covered by health insurance, you generally have no choice: the standard form that most companies require you to sign will authorize the release to them of medical records, including therapy. What's more, under many plans therapy must be authorized by a company representative, a process that may require you to discuss your problems, over the phone, with a stranger who may or may not have mental health training.

This is an area of considerable contemporary controversy, which will be discussed at greater length. But it is reasonable to expect that the health insurer's right to know about your therapy has limits.

When asked by your insurer about your treatment, your therapist should not reveal any more than is necessary—for example, the diagnosis, prognosis, and expected duration. This limitation to the revelation of the least information necessary is a matter of law in some states.

Every relationship has its own idiosyncrasies, and therapy is no exception. Energy devoted at the outset to clarifying nuts-and-bolts arrangements, airing expectations, and eliminating misunderstandings will be well invested.

**Time.** The duration of each session should be clear (the "therapy hour" is generally forty-five to fifty minutes), along with the matter of fees, manner of payment, and policy on missed sessions. In traditional psychoanalysis and much therapy, it used to be customary for the patient to pay for all his scheduled sessions, even those he was forced to cancel. The patient only took a vacation from therapy when the therapist did (traditionally in August).

The rationale was twofold: when the going got tough, according to theory, the patient was tempted to stay home. Allowing free cancellations, even for apparently legitimate reasons, did a disservice by making it too easy to avoid coming to grips with painful emotions and difficult material. At the same time, the reasoning went, this policy was only fair to the analyst, who had set the time aside and would be unable to fill it otherwise.

Some therapists may still insist on this arrangement, or modifications of it (e.g., you can switch to another time slot, if one is available, when you must miss your scheduled session). But they are a dwindling minority. The American Psychiatric Association's guidelines, in fact, say that while charging for a missed session isn't necessarily unethical, it should be "resorted to infrequently."

Far more common nowadays is a policy of charging for a missed or canceled session only if you fail to notify the therapist twenty-four hours in advance—similar to the office policy of many physicians and other professionals. Some will be flexible if the session is missed because of an unforeseeable mishap (such as a subway breakdown). Whatever the arrangement, it should be explicit—especially if your job requires intermittent travel. (Note: Don't expect your therapist to bill your insurance company for a missed therapy session; this would constitute fraud.)

**Contact between sessions.** Some therapists are amenable to ad hoc telephone counseling in times of crisis; others are stricter. If you leave a message on her answering machine, how soon can you expect a call back? Communication by e-mail has become increasingly common in health care, including therapy. Establish what subject matter is appropriate for electronic messages, keeping in mind that confidentiality is impossible to guarantee under these circumstances.

Speaking of confidentiality, it's a good idea to discuss in advance just how much information the therapist will share with your health insurance company and with any other parties that have a right to it. You may want spelled out the conditions under which confidentiality can be broken, and specify that you wish to be notified whenever this happens.

**Identifying goals.** Among the dimensions of the therapy process you might want to establish at the outset are: What do you hope to accomplish in therapy? What is the treatment plan? How long will it take?

How precisely these questions are answered will vary enormously, depending on the kind of therapy and the circumstances under which it is taking place. A highly focused approach, such as cognitive therapy, may specify the diagnosis, goals, and treatment plan very explicitly; especially when insurance is involved, the length of therapy may be defined as well.

Many professionals, however, regard the therapy process in a more fluid way, as a work in progress whose direction can be sketched out but not rigidly charted in advance. The therapist may propose an outline of what he expects to happen, but new goals are likely to emerge as therapy proceeds, and estimates of time are subject to constant revision. One question you have every right to pose, however, is "How soon might I expect to feel better?"

In recent years, an increasing number of psychotherapists have begun to put much of this in writing, with an "informed consent" letter that outlines what you're getting into when you enter therapy, the potential risks and benefits, and the contractual obligations on both sides. This kind of document has long been a part of medical practice, particularly when surgery or other procedures are involved.

Although written consent is still the exception in therapy, don't be surprised if your new therapist presents you with such a letter. But remember that informed consent is a process, not an event; like any contract, it is subject to discussion and usually requires clarification. An informed consent letter should initiate a dialogue about your therapy but doesn't take its place.

# Chapter 4

—

# SCIENCE AND PSYCHOTHERAPY

## The Lessons of Research

You might think of psychotherapy as a big, sometimes contentious tribe of individuals who have a broadly common purpose but who differ in their beliefs and in the methods they choose to achieve their ends. The members of the tribe are all somehow related, some showing an unmistakable family resemblance, others sharing distant ancestry. There are four hundred types of therapy, according to estimates cited in the surgeon general's *Mental Health* report. But most of these are actually variations on a few basic themes.

What most therapists practice is some form (or combination) of three kinds of therapy: psychodynamic, behavioral, and humanistic. You may receive therapy as an individual, as part of a group, or along with other members of your family or someone with whom you are in an important relationship. Virtually any kind of therapy can be short-term—five, ten, or twenty sessions—or long-term, perhaps lasting for years.

Does it really matter what kind of therapy you choose? This may seem an impertinent question, in light of all the time and energy that has been invested in developing, honing, and writing about theory and practice in the field. But the issue is actually far from settled. Only recently have the kinds of scientific standards used in testing medications been applied to therapy. And there is no consensus about the results.

The discussion that follows goes into some detail about this research. It is intended to clarify issues that may come up when choosing between different kinds of therapy. If you aren't much interested in technicalities, you may want to go directly to chapters that describe the therapies themselves. But keep these points in mind:

• Most people who have therapy are satisfied with the outcome, and report similar gains whether they see a psychiatrist, psychologist, or social worker. In general surveys, no one kind of therapy has been shown to be superior to others.

• When types of therapy are examined more scientifically, there is plenty of evidence to support the effectiveness of some, very little for others.

• But these findings are not the last word. Certain types of therapy are simply easier to study scientifically than others. If there is little data to back up a therapy, it could just mean that it hasn't been examined in rigorous trials.

• Success under "laboratory conditions" is not the same as effectiveness in the real world. The way patients are chosen and therapy is given, even the personal beliefs of the experimenter, may influence the outcome.

• No study can say which therapy is going to work best for any one individual. While research can be a useful guide, it shouldn't take the place of personal preference and experience.

What the authors called "the dodo bird verdict" (after the caucus-race episode in *Alice's Adventures in Wonderland,* where the dodo concludes that "*everybody* has won and all must have prizes") was the outcome of a classic comparison of psychotherapies in 1975: no one school of therapy emerged as consistently better than the others.

Twenty years and many psychotherapies later, a study by *Consumer Reports* came to a very similar conclusion. The magazine sent a survey to 180,000 of its readers, which was returned by 7,000 who had sought help (from friends, family, clergy, support groups, physicians, or mental health professionals) for stress or other emotional problems within the previous three years. Of these, 2,900 had gone to mental health professionals, and most of these felt significantly better by the time of the survey.

The study found that most licensed therapists were comparably effective: respondents reported similar gains whether they saw a psychologist, social worker, or psychiatrist. Those who brought their problems to marriage counselors didn't report quite as much benefit, however.

What's more, the results were similar regardless of the type of therapy administered for any given problem. A depressed person, that is, felt she benefited comparably whether she had psychodynamic therapy or cognitive-behavioral therapy, and whether or not she took medication at the same time.

Among the weaknesses of the study were the lack of control groups for comparison (people with similar problems who had no therapy at all) and the fact that findings were based on subjective opinion rather than objective tests. Although the report carried the positive message that most people who saw most therapists for most problems were pretty much satisfied with the results, it couldn't say with scientific accuracy which psychotherapies were best for which people, and whether some truly worked while others didn't.

In recent years, researchers have attempted to answer such questions with more rigorously designed studies, *clinical trials* in which patients are randomly assigned to receive specific kinds of therapy or none at all. This attempt to establish "evidence-based psychotherapy" is similar to efforts that have subjected medical treatments, many of them used for generations simply because they appeared to work, to a more scientific standard of proof.

The problem, some argue, is that randomized controlled trials are not as neatly applicable to psychotherapy as medications. Making sure that all the participants in a study receive the same kind of therapy usually requires therapists to follow a detailed manual of techniques, and this can be done more readily with some modes of therapy than others. And it is difficult and expensive to apply this kind of testing to anything other than short-term therapy. Most clinical trials last six to twelve weeks, but some kinds of therapy go on for a year or longer.

Treatments that seem quite effective in scientific studies may be less impressive in the real world, a disparity that the U.S. surgeon general's *Mental Health* report calls the gap between "efficacy" (what works in clinical trials) and "effectiveness" (what works in typical practice).

This may be because experimental conditions are ideal in a way that sets them apart from real experience. People with multiple problems make up a substantial proportion of therapy seekers, but they are usually eliminated from clinical trials, which strive, for simplicity, to isolate a uniform group (patients who are depressed, for example, but have no other diagnoses). And many other people seek help for vague but troubling complaints ("Things just don't seem right") that don't fit any diagnosis at all.

Therapists in clinical trials are often better trained to do the therapy under study than those in the community, and patients are followed more carefully than usual and are more likely to follow instructions faithfully. Therapy is generally given free of charge, which eliminates the pressures and constraints that may influence the length and intensity of care under real-life conditions.

Most people seeking help choose a therapist and type of therapy they find congenial, but scientific studies usually demand random assignment. And effective therapy in the real world tends to be flexible—the therapist matches her approach to the individual and adjusts it if things aren't working—while this isn't allowed in a clinical trial.

Even well-designed research studies may be influenced by the theories of the researcher. A 1999 analysis in the journal *Clinical Psychology: Science and Practice* considered twenty-nine clinical trials where one type of therapy was compared with another, and found that the treatment favored by the researcher (as inferred from articles he had written, the researcher's own account of his theoretical beliefs, and the opinions of colleagues) was significantly more likely to come out superior. The "allegiance effect" in this study explained more than two thirds of the reported difference between treatments.

Still and all, randomized controlled trials have provided information that you might want to take into account when making choices about therapy. In depression, for example, they support the use of cognitive-behavioral therapy and interpersonal therapy (these approaches were about as effective as drugs in one large, well-designed study sponsored by the National Institute of Mental Health) but provide less backing for other therapies. In the treatment of anxiety disorders, certain kinds of highly focused, problem-oriented therapy have consistently emerged ahead of therapy that aims to help patients change by fostering insight into the sources of their painful feelings.

If you're interested in reviewing what the experts have to say about therapy and drug treatment for many common emotional disorders, check the practice guidelines published by the American Psychiatric Association [www.psych.org/clin_res/prac_guide.cfm]. These are written for professionals and are rather technical, so extracting material meaningful for you could take some digging.

More consumer-oriented treatment information is available in "A Guide to Beneficial Therapy," put together by the clinical psychology division of the American Psychological Association [www.apa.org/divisions/div12/rev_est/index.shtml]. For a number of common disorders, including anxiety, stress, depression, eating disorders, and substance abuse, it lists and describes the treatments that have been shown effective in randomized controlled trials.

The psychologists who assembled this information recommend that patients seek therapies that have been shown effective in scientific studies, but they also grant that often, a treatment that does not appear in the lists simply hasn't been subjected to scientific scrutiny, rather than tested and found wanting. And that no study, no matter how well designed, can say whether a particular treatment will help a particular person under the care of a particular therapist.

One conclusion supported by a number of studies is that more is better, at least some of the time, and for some people. In the *Consumer Reports* survey, people who continued in therapy for more than six months reported more improvement and satisfaction with treatment than those who stayed for a shorter time. Another study found that half of the patients had made measurable gains after eight sessions of various kinds of therapy, compared with three fourths after twenty-six sessions. On the other hand, a law of diminishing returns seems to operate: improvements are usually more dramatic early in therapy, and gradual later on.

The more severe your problems, unsurprisingly, the more therapy you're likely to need to make a difference, particularly if they are chronic, like feelings of worthlessness, loneliness, and hostility, as opposed to acute symptoms, like restlessness and crying. And after you've gotten well, a bit of extra care, perhaps in the form of periodic "booster" sessions, appears to make it less likely that a condition like depression will come back.

The bottom line seems to be that while there are some general guidelines about what kind and how much therapy is most likely to be helpful, the individual factor can't be eliminated. For those people in the study cited above who got better quickly, eight sessions were enough. But others, perhaps with what looked like similar problems, needed more.

Writing in the *Harvard Mental Health Letter,* Jacqueline B. Persons, Ph.D., a psychologist at the University of California, San Diego, proposed that therapists "adapt the treatment to the patient's individual needs in a systematic fashion, as if the therapy were a scientific experiment with a sample of one." If progress isn't satisfactory, both patient and therapist should be ready to change treatment plans and try new approaches.

In practice, most therapists nowadays tend to be "eclectic"; they combine elements from different schools of therapy, tailoring what they do to the unique problems of each person in their care. "There is a large—and rapidly growing—cadre of therapists who seek to move beyond the confining strictures of ideology," writes Paul Wachtel, Ph.D., a professor of psychology at the City University of New York.

Often it appears that psychotherapists start out with a sharply focused orientation shaped by their training, but as they grow in experience their outlook becomes more flexible. "We learn what works, and keep on doing it," says a psychologist who has been in practice for thirty years.

At the same time, the divisions between different kinds of therapy are less distinct than they once were. Modern forms of cognitive therapy, which largely focuses on "here and now" thoughts and behavior, pay more attention to a patient's past than older versions did, for example. And psychodynamic approaches have broadened to deal with the role of interpersonal relationships and conscious thoughts as well as unconscious conflicts.

Therapies still differ in their conception of the mind, their sense of what's important in life, and their version of what goes wrong and how to put it right. Some emphasize introspection or experience, some the building of skills or the development of insight. Does the therapist "cure" a disorder the way a doctor treats an infection, or strive to facilitate your own innate capacity for growth? Does she set a specific agenda and keep you on track, or simply create an atmosphere in which you can explore?

What makes most sense to you? Choosing a therapist whose approach and worldview are in keeping with your own could be as important as research results when it comes to getting what you want out of therapy.

## Chapter 5

—

# WHAT LIES BENEATH

*Psychoanalysis and Psychodynamic Therapy*

It's hardly an exaggeration to say that psychotherapy started with Sigmund Freud. Roughly a century ago the Viennese physician developed a theory of how the mind works and a way of treating emotional problems by bringing these workings into the light: the original "talking cure."

In the years since, Freud has been idolized and vilified, emulated and attacked. His theories have been discussed reverently and dismissed as pernicious nonsense, but rarely ignored and never forgotten. Although his original approach, *psychoanalysis,* is practiced (in a modified form) by a minority of therapists today, the principles and techniques he pioneered continue to exert a definitive influence. Much of today's psychotherapy either evolved from Freud's psychoanalysis—what is called "psychodynamic therapy"—or as a reaction against it.

Freud's most important contribution, perhaps, was a highly original map of the mind, a complex conception of human nature that many agree has had a profound impact on twentieth-century culture unrivaled by other systems of psychology. Its influence is so pervasive that we use psychodynamic concepts without even thinking:

when we talk of "repression," "defenses," or "unconscious" wishes, when we forget an appointment and wonder whether we really didn't want to go.

Put simply, psychoanalysis proposed that mental life is largely shaped by instincts, such as the drive to have pleasure and avoid pain, and by experiences in the first few years of life—and that the long-ago past continues to play a dominant role in the feelings and actions of today. It sees the mind as a structure, in dynamic tension among elements that blindly seek to gratify instincts (the "id"), that operate rationally to protect the self (the "ego"), and that serve as a conscience or brake to maintain control (the "superego").

Perhaps most important, it suggests that the vast bulk of our mental life takes place beneath the surface and outside our awareness: it is "unconscious." And that images, events, and contending forces in the unconscious are largely responsible for the ways we feel and act—and for the kinds of troubles that bring us into therapy.

The goal of psychoanalysis—and to a great extent of the psychodynamic therapies that come from it—is to make us aware of what goes on in the unconscious, and so to release ourselves from its tyranny.

While psychoanalysis originally concerned itself with "intrapsychic" matters—the structure of and forces within the mind of the individual—its modern-day descendants pay at least as much attention to the way you interact with others: the quality of your relationships, how you see yourself and those who are important to you, and how these patterns can be modified in a satisfying way.

## How It Works

"Psychodynamic psychotherapy" is a broad term, embracing varied approaches that take its basic premises in different directions. In its purest form, *psychoanalysis,* the patient, or "analysand," comes in three or more times a week, usually for a number of years. The therapist (more properly, the "analyst") is nondirective—she listens to the patient and makes conjectures about the significance of what he says ("interpretations") but does not offer suggestions about what to talk about next, much less give advice about how to run his life.

*Psychodynamic therapy,* which is far more common, involves one, perhaps two visits a week, for a period of weeks, months, or years. The therapist uses many of the same techniques as the analyst (discussed at length below) but may not feel bound to remain in a purely nondirective role. She may more actively keep the subject on course (to deal with a particular problem, for example) and even make concrete suggestions that are applicable to the patient's life outside the treatment room.

Psychodynamic therapy may even be primarily *supportive,* attempting to help the patient mobilize her existing strengths in dealing with life problems, rather than challenging her defenses in order to unearth the unconscious wishes and fears that caused the problems. This kind of therapy is often of limited duration, perhaps in a time of crisis, but may be ongoing for people with serious mental problems.

People come into psychodynamic therapy for all the usual reasons, whether specific—something has gone wrong in a relationship, they have difficulty at work, have alienated friends by angry outbursts, or are plagued with anxiety or so depressed that it's difficult to work or sleep—or something as vague as simply feeling "hollow inside." The therapy aims to address the problem but differs from other approaches by seeing the immediate situation in a broader, deeper context—a reflection of patterns and forces that have been operating throughout the patient's life.

"The first goal is to see if the person wants to explore what issues in his past life might be relevant to his present troubles," says Leon Hoffman, M.D., chair of the public-information committee of the American Psychoanalytic Association. To profit from this approach, you must be ready to consider that life is being made difficult by something brewing within, not just external circumstances like a bad job market or a shortage of appropriate men.

In seeking the roots of the problem, the therapist will probably devote a good deal of energy to exploring *conflicts*—between conscious and unconscious needs, wishes, and fears, between safety and desire. A person may want to make friends, connect with others, express his ideas. But for reasons of which he probably is not aware, this seems "dangerous"—it threatens him with loss, shame, or injury. The result can be anxiety.

Another key concept is that of *defenses.* To keep wishes or fantasies that would arouse painful emotions like shame, anxiety, or guilt out of consciousness, to protect the self from feeling overwhelmed, the unconscious mind uses strategies like *displacement* (it's dangerous to recognize your anger at your boss, so you feel angry at your husband instead); *projection* (you were taught at an early age that it's unacceptable for you to need attention, so you experience others as needy and demanding); or *intellectualization* (you've learned to see your life clearly, but coldly—you can precisely say what's gone wrong with a relationship, but somehow you don't feel the pain).

As a consequence of your mind's attempts to protect itself, you may have adopted patterns of behavior and feeling that allow you to maintain a safe sense of equilibrium, but at a cost. You find it impossible to get truly close to others or to put yourself wholeheartedly into your work, or you somehow sabotage your attempts to succeed. Time and again, you make the same mistake.

From a psychodynamic point of view, the way out of this dilemma is to bring the underlying forces to light—to make the unconscious (and largest) portion of the drama conscious. But this is not a simple undertaking, or a quick one. The same forces that sent certain needs, fears, and desires into the unconscious act to keep them there. The mind's bastion is not unassailable, however—if approached with patience and skill, it yields up its secrets in bits and pieces.

One technique that is central in psychoanalysis and important in much psychodynamic therapy is *free association.* You are encouraged to let your attention drift and to say "whatever comes to mind." This unfocused state weakens logical connections, lulls defenses, allows fleeting glimpses of the mental life that is otherwise kept under wraps. Promoting free association is a principal reason that traditional psychoanalysis (and some psychodynamic therapy) is conducted while the patient lies on a couch (another being that Freud, by his own admission, found it difficult to be stared at by patients, one after another, for eight hours a day).

Dreams are, as Freud famously said, "the royal road to the unconscious," and his book *The Interpretation of Dreams* is a landmark of psychoanalysis. Events, people, and objects in dreams enact the drama of inner conflict in concrete form, expressing wishes that, awake, we would never put into words. Contrary to the popular image, the therapist does not interpret a dream as if deciphering a coded message with a fixed system of symbols. Rather, interpretation is a collaborative effort in which the dreamer takes the leading role, in part through free association, gradually unraveling the subtext that the dream contains.

To allow the unconscious to express itself, psychodynamic therapy tends to be less structured than other approaches. When you come in for your session, the therapist will very likely say little until you begin, and if you don't know *where* to begin, the silence may extend for some time. The agenda is open, and you're the one to set it, which can create the same feeling of anxiety—and perhaps excitement—that a writer feels facing a blank page. It can be an uncomfortable space, but one in which unexpected things happen and important discoveries are made.

The role of the therapist in this process is subtle and easily misunderstood. Traditionally, she is to remain "neutral"—a word that may summon up the image of an impassive analyst, a silent, uninvolved witness to the patient's struggles. But that is a stereotype that has little relevance today. The therapist doesn't withdraw her personality but keeps it in the background; she stays out of the way while remaining very definitely "there."

This studied neutrality promotes the development of *transference*—the projection of feelings that you originally had for your parents (or other key figures from your early life) onto the therapist.

Transference is a pervasive phenomenon, according to psychodynamic theory, and by no means limited to therapy—students often fall in love with their teachers and patients follow (or flout) their doctors' orders not because of the qualities these people possess, but because the authority, respect, or power they command awakens echoes of the past. Personal relationships are also shaped (and misshapen) by long-ago feelings.

Transference, in other words, is everywhere. But only in therapy are the conditions expressly designed to give you the opportunity to recognize it, analyze it, and understand where it comes from—and so free yourself from its underground influence. In fact the feelings you have for your therapist are often an important theme in psychodynamic therapy, if not a preoccupation.

More generally, how you feel and behave in the therapy room is likely to come under close scrutiny. Come in late to your session, and another type of therapist may simply ask you to do better, but here the possible meaning behind your "carelessness" can be the subject of an entire session. The situation is a kind of laboratory where you bring the same patterns of thought, feeling, and behavior that run throughout your life and that show the marks of your earliest years. In a session, attention may range back and forth, making connections between the immediate situation, events and relationships in your "real life" outside of therapy, and the past.

A skilled therapist doesn't force these connections on you but furthers the process through *interpretations,* offering hypotheses and drawing tentative conclusions from what you are saying. There's an art to it, which includes knowing when and how to bring up matters that you're avoiding, and carefully phrasing comments and asking questions that lead you to clarify and reach the insights toward which you may be struggling. Timing, tone, and subtlety are crucial.

While insight is necessary for progress in therapy, it isn't sufficient. It is possible, actually, for a connection to be made that leads in a fairly direct line to a change in behavior. A man realizes, in the middle of ranting at his therapist, that he sounds *exactly* the way his father did during the temper outbursts that he hated. And he stops doing it. But this is, to put it mildly, very rare.

The rule is that insight is followed by a period, sometimes quite lengthy, of *working through*—bringing what starts out as an intellectual discovery, an abstraction, to life. Taking the insight, in the words of one psychologist, "from the neck up to the neck down." Making it part of you. It's a learning process, a gradual integration in which the same discovery is made in different situations, over and over. The angry man must lose his temper with his wife, with his children, with a toll collector, again and again, before he *feels* the connection with his early life that will ultimately enable him to choose how to deal with his impulses, which in turn will give him a new measure of control over his actions.

There are other reasons why the path of therapy rarely runs smooth. The human tendency to avoid pain isn't suspended just because you've decided to get down to business and change your life. And this kind of therapy inevitably demands facing feelings, fears, and fantasies that you've stayed away from *because* they are painful. Eager as you may consciously be to seek insights and confront your demons, there's an unconscious part of you that will go to great lengths to do anything else.

This *resistance* can range from forgetting to show up for a session to forgetting everything said in a session, from dismissing all the therapist's interpretations as foolishness (while staying in therapy with him) to agreeing wholeheartedly with everything he says (but somehow never putting it into action), to constantly finding it pressing to talk about matters that have to do with anything else. After you've recognized an insight, there may still be considerable resistance to working it through. Any change, even change for the better, involves some loss.

Don't get the idea that resistance is a *bad* thing. From the point of view of therapy, it's particularly promising material to be analyzed, more "grist for the mill" that may provide valuable opportunities for new interpretations and insights. Resistance reflects the operation of defenses that you use to keep anxiety at bay; looking at it analytically can show you these defenses in action—an important step in getting past them to confront the issues that cause you trouble.

While the relationship with the therapist is important in any kind of therapy, here it is absolutely central. As discussed above, it's a subject, often the single most pervasive subject, of the therapy itself. Transference is likely to be strong—intentionally so, to provide material for interpretation—but if it includes strongly negative feelings, like anger, dismissal, or contempt, and these aren't handled deftly, this can prove a fatal barrier to the therapeutic alliance that enables you and the therapist to work together.

The alliance is particularly critical in view of the difficult material that comes up in psychodynamic therapy. Ideally, therapy constructs "a safe place" where you can explore issues that arouse anxiety and take risks by talking about things that make you feel guilty, ashamed, or threatened. British psychiatrist D. W. Winnicott suggested that therapy creates a "holding environment," analogous to the feeling of safety and comfort that a mother creates for a young child, in which he can test his developing powers, grow and extend his range.

The therapeutic relationship can be healing in its own right, offering a "corrective emotional experience" of dependability, generosity, and acceptance that helps to redress past hurts. The benevolent figure of the therapist can replace the image of a threatening, belittling, or demanding parent in your mind, changing the internal model that cast a shadow over the way you have seen people throughout your adult life.

The intensity generated by the closeness of therapy can also arouse strong feelings in the therapist—including some that tap into her own past experience. Here she herself becomes a "laboratory" where feelings aren't acted upon but are analyzed: she can interpret this *countertransference* to understand, through dispassionate observation of herself, the feelings that a patient arouses in others.

The ability to recognize and use countertransference therapeutically requires a high degree of self-awareness. There are compelling reasons why psychoanalysts must be analyzed themselves, as part of their training, and why most therapists who practice psychodynamic therapy have invested sufficient time in their own therapy to understand where their feelings come from and how to deal with them in a way that helps—or at least doesn't hinder—their work. How much therapy she has had is an appropriate question for your initial consultation with a prospective therapist.

## Therapy Long and Short

Traditional dynamic therapy is open-ended, following a sometimes wandering course along the contours of unconscious conflicts and issues as they reveal themselves. It stops, starts, runs into roadblocks as it evolves at its own, sometimes glacial pace.

Therapists who work this way resist setting a timetable for their efforts: no one can say how long it takes for free association to lead to insight, or what resistances will arise. "It's like asking how long it will take to walk around the block," says Ted A. Grossbart, Ph.D., assistant clinical professor of psychology at Harvard Medical School. "That depends on how fast you walk, whether you stop for coffee, chat with neighbors, or pause to enjoy the view."

How far you go in analysis or therapy is largely a matter of individual goals. Do you simply want to resolve an immediate crisis and return to the way you lived before, or do you hope to confront difficulties that have long made life less than you want? A man who seeks therapy because he's depressed over the ending of a love affair may stay to explore the forces behind a long history of unsuccessful relationships. Some analysts consider their approach strongest in dealing with problems that have a long history: chronic, ongoing life dissatisfaction and the deeply embedded character problems that cause continuing relationship difficulties and self-destructive behavior.

"In psychoanalysis, patients often end up changing immense things in their lives . . . they adjust huge areas of functioning," says

Barbara Milrod, M.D., a psychiatrist at Joan and Sanford I. Weill Medical College, Cornell University. Past a certain point, it's less a matter of relieving "symptoms" than of following the ancient dictum "Know thyself," which explains the traditional appeal of psychoanalysis to people who take an interest in exploring human nature: artists, writers, intellectuals.

Particularly today, this open-ended quality is a drawback as well as a strength. Self-knowledge is not a compelling motive to health insurance companies; most people who seek psychoanalysis, and many in long-term psychodynamic therapy, pay the cost out-of-pocket. And many want quicker results, even if it leaves the subtleties of personality largely unexplored.

*Brief dynamic therapies* address these issues by applying analytic concepts in an accelerated format. While *brief* is a relative term, they generally operate within a framework of twenty-five sessions or less. As important as time is the restriction in focus: brief dynamic therapy chooses a central theme or problem—difficulties with anger, perhaps, or a recurrent pattern that interferes with personal relationships—and the therapist takes a more active role in keeping the therapy on target.

The role of childhood experiences in generating conflicts and problem patterns is still an object of attention, but here the focus never ranges far from life in the present. Transference too remains important, but it is analyzed more quickly than in extended therapy—particularly when it takes the form of negative feelings that could slow down the work. The therapist makes a conscious effort to keep the patient from developing dependence, by maintaining an emphasis on her strengths.

Although brief therapy has economic appeal (particularly when insurance companies are footing the bill), it has theoretical justification as well. Proponents note that when both patient and therapist know that time is limited, the process of therapy is accelerated, and research suggests that a sharper focus on specific themes may improve the outcome. Some point out that most people limit the length of therapy on their own, and are less likely to drop out prematurely when the term has been set in advance.

Most studies have shown time-limited therapy to be no less effective than the traditional open-ended approach.

## What Dynamic Therapy Works For

There is very little hard scientific evidence that dynamic therapy is effective. This does not constitute proof that the approach doesn't work: for the most part, rigorous tests haven't been applied, for a number of reasons.

To be studied scientifically, a therapy must be prescribed in step-by-step detail in a manual and administered in the same way by all participating therapists. Dynamic therapy resists this approach because it takes a different course with each patient. "Its hallmark is an individualized relationship between you and the therapist," Dr. Hoffman says. "The aim isn't just general symptom relief, but dealing with issues that are unique to you."

In addition, therapy that lasts for years (as traditional psychodynamic approaches do) is far more difficult to study than therapy of several months' duration. And historically, psychoanalysts have written about their work in case studies—highly detailed descriptions of specific patients and their treatment—rather than by comparing groups of patients who have had therapy with those who have not.

The American Psychological Association lists psychodynamic therapy as "possibly effective" for certain anxiety disorders, depression, and opiate addiction. It is one of the two specific therapies described in some detail in the American Psychiatric Association's *Practice Guideline for the Treatment of Panic Disorder,* but that document specifies that "there are no published reports of randomized controlled trials evaluating the efficacy of this approach" for the condition. Some open studies—trials without a control group—have been promising, however. One recently found that twenty-four sessions of brief dynamic therapy were as effective in reducing panic symptoms as medication and other recognized therapies had been in earlier studies.

The APA's *Practice Guideline for Major Depressive Disorder* notes that psychodynamic psychotherapies "have not been subjected to controlled studies" but that many case reports suggest their value. (In particular, they may help patients whose depression is linked to perfectionism.) Other APA guidelines suggest that dynamic therapies may be useful in anorexia and bulimia nervosa, perhaps preventing relapse by addressing personality conflicts once symptoms are under control; and that case studies suggest their possible value for substance abuse.

One recent study of particular interest compared patients with borderline personality disorder who received an intensive program of psychoanalytic therapy with others who had standard psychiatric care. Those who participated in the program were less depressed and anxious and were less likely to injure themselves after eighteen months of treatment. What's more, they showed additional improvement when evaluated eighteen months after treatment had ended.

## Finding a Psychodynamic Therapist

Many therapists incorporate psychodynamic principles into their work, and someone who describes himself as "eclectic" very likely will use some of the techniques described above. If you're interested in psychoanalysis itself, or in therapy that is explicitly based on psychodynamic principles, you may want to see a therapist who has had more extensive training in this field.

A graduate of a *psychoanalytic institute* has gone through a course of study that includes analyzing a patient under the close supervision of an experienced analyst and has himself undergone a "training analysis" as part of the program. If the person is licensed as a psychiatrist, psychologist, or social worker, she also has had the full training necessary for those credentials.

Although graduates of psychoanalytic institutes perform psychoanalysis, virtually all do less intensive, shorter-term therapy as well.

A listing of many such graduates, by state, can be found at the website of the American Psychoanalytic Association [http://apsa.org].

Most psychoanalytic institutes maintain community clinics, which provide low-cost psychoanalysis and psychodynamic therapy, often by training candidates who are already experienced therapists. Fees are usually charged on a sliding scale, depending on your income. Links to many such institutes can be found at the websites of Psyche Matters [www.psychematters.com/psainst.htm] or the American Psychoanalytic Foundation [www.cyberpsych.org/apf/links.html].

## Chapter 6

—

# DOING AND THINKING

## *Cognitive and Behavioral Therapies*

In recent decades, therapies have come into prominence that depart markedly from the psychoanalytic script. Instead of unconscious instincts, processes, and conflicts, they focus on aspects of our lives that are more immediately accessible, *behavior* and *cognition*—how we act and how we think—and apply strategies to modify them directly.

Cognitive and behavioral therapies represent two streams of development that have largely but not entirely merged. They have much in common. Both are far more goal-oriented than traditional psychodynamic therapy; they have well-defined objectives and are generally more limited in duration; they are more structured and planned; and they stress the importance of close—one might say "scientific"—observation and assessment of the individual and his problems.

While some therapists call themselves "behavioral" and some "cognitive," most who work in this way actually combine elements of both approaches. Within the broad category of cognitive-behavioral therapy there's room for different strategies, emphases, and schools. So it's wise to establish at the start just how a particular therapist works and what he plans to do.

## Behavior Therapy

The roots of the behavioral approach to therapy are in experimental science and go back to animal studies of the nineteenth and early twentieth centuries. It is based in the idea of learning—how animals (including humans) change the way they act in response to their environment.

Perhaps the most familiar example of behaviorism is represented by the work of Ivan Pavlov, the Russian scientist who illuminated the workings of *classical conditioning:* a dog who is fed whenever a bell rings will learn to salivate when the bell is rung, even if he is not fed. The dog has been conditioned to associate the sound of the bell with the appearance of food, and his body reacts accordingly.

A similar but more active process is *operant conditioning,* which occurs when the actions of an animal (or person) in its environment makes something happen. A positive consequence (reinforcement) makes it more likely that the action will be repeated, while a negative one (punishment) makes it less likely; through such experiences, you *learn* to behave in a certain way.

To take a simple example, if adults repeatedly respond to a child's tantrums by giving her a cookie or a soothing word, she will probably learn to behave differently over time (and perhaps as an adult) than if she is reprimanded or ignored when she behaves in an overly demanding way.

Until the middle of the twentieth century, behavioral psychologists maintained a rigorously scientific focus on physical behavior. Like scientists in other fields, they accepted as "real" only phenomena that could be shown objectively to exist. To them, "anxiety" might be defined in terms of things that could be seen and measured—a rapid heart rate, shallow breathing, defensive posture, sweating. To the person who is actually having an anxiety attack, a highly unpleasant set of thoughts, emotions, and bodily sensations might seem to be the essence of the experience. But because these private realities cannot be objectively verified, they would have no place in a scientific definition acceptable to behaviorists.

From a strictly behaviorist point of view, a person is essentially the product of his environment; as complex as human behavior may seem, it can ultimately be explained as a bundle of conditioned responses. This is a view that many regard as pessimistic, reducing such highly prized and distinctively human attributes as self-determination and freedom to illusions whose origins can be traced back to the primitive laws that govern learning throughout the animal kingdom.

In recent decades, however, behaviorists have expanded their outlook, coming to see humans in a more reciprocal, dynamic relationship with their environment; we shape our world as well as being shaped by it. Modern behavioral psychologists regard thoughts and feelings as types of events and behavior, subject to the same laws as physical actions and reactions and molded by the same processes of conditioning.

Today, relatively few therapists restrict their activities to a radically behaviorist format—that is, with strict attention to what people do and none to how they think and feel. But many use techniques that derive quite directly from the insights and theories of the behaviorists.

One simple behavioral strategy is *relaxation training,* in which you might be taught to induce a deeply relaxed state by breathing deeply, visualizing a peaceful scene, or loosening your muscles one by one. With practice, the connection between the exercise and the relaxed state becomes strong and automatic—you can achieve a degree of relaxation virtually at will, even in the turmoil of daily life. This can be extremely useful for stress control and in the treatment of physical disorders (such as headache and back pain) that are caused or worsened by tension.

From a behavioral point of view, anxiety is largely the result of conditioning; in a simple phobia, for example, you have learned to associate an object or situation with intense fear. In its treatment, relaxation training may be enlisted as part of a broader strategy called *systematic desensitization,* which exploits the fact that conditioning can be *inhibited* by substituting a new response for the anxiety that had come to be associated with the object.

If you have a phobia about cats, for example, you may be instructed to imagine a scene where a very small cat is at a distance, while you are in a state of deep relaxation that inhibits the fear response. Gradually, you imagine more and more frightening scenarios (a large cat, perhaps, in a small room), then experience a graded sequence of real-life situations, as the relaxation state prevents anxiety from kicking in. Ultimately, you should be able to stroke a real cat calmly and even with pleasure.

*Assertiveness training* uses related principles to teach people to stand up for their rights in an effective way. Here the anxiety characteristically felt in a situation where assertion is called for is inhibited by activity: when you actually speak up, the anxiety dissipates. Not only is this approach helpful for people whose timidity gets in the way of their lives, it can be effective when anger control is the problem; if you learn to deal with frustrations and irritations in a firm but reasonable way as they come up, rage will not build to the point of explosion.

A further refinement of this technique uses the fact that conditioning is subject to *extinction:* if you are repeatedly exposed to a stimulus and the response does not occur, the connection will gradually dwindle of its own accord. *Exposure therapy* enlists this process with increasing "doses" of the object of anxiety, leaving out the relaxation component. For example, you may start out in the room with a picture of a cat, then with a small cat in a cage, and so on, each time experiencing, with the aid of the therapist, that the feared consequences simply don't happen.

A therapist may become involved in this kind of therapy in a highly active way: accompanying a patient with a fear of crossing bridges, for example, as he drives across a small bridge, then larger ones. She may also provide a model, by approaching and stroking an animal that the patient fears, as a first step toward treating a phobia.

*Biofeedback,* a term that is familiar to many people, represents a kind of technologically enhanced application of behavioral principles. It employs a device that monitors a physiological process (like heart rate, blood pressure, or muscle tension), and emits a signal (usually an audible tone) to reveal how it changes—for example, when blood pressure rises or falls. The guided use of the device helps you learn to control processes of which you're normally unaware. Biofeedback has been useful in stress and anxiety conditions, especially when physical symptoms like headache or back pain are involved.

*Hypnosis,* in which the therapist guides you to experience reality differently, may be employed to enhance behavioral techniques like relaxation and distraction, and to help you mentally rehearse more effective ways of dealing with problem situations. It has been particularly useful for medical conditions that cause chronic pain or where stress is a factor.

## Cognitive-Behavioral Therapy

While behavioral psychologists were beginning to incorporate thought and feeling into their concept of human nature, another school of thought was moving into similar territory from a different direction. The key figures in *cognitive therapy* and *rational emotive therapy,* Aaron Beck, M.D., and Albert Ellis, Ph.D., were trained in psychoanalytic theory and developed their approaches out of dissatisfaction with it.

The methods devised by figures like Beck, Ellis, and others diverge from one another in a number of ways but have in common the premise that individuals don't merely react to a reality that we all share; rather, each actively *constructs* his own world through his thoughts, beliefs, and assumptions. As human beings, we are inexorably driven to find meaning in our world and our lives, and this cognitive enterprise is a fundamental human task. Some cognitive-behavioral therapists speak of the "stories" that we create to organize the events of our lives into a meaningful structure.

Our emotions and behavior emerge in reaction to this world—the one that we make for ourselves—and if these feelings and actions cause problems, it is because the reality we create is distorted or dysfunctional. While the whole idea of psychotherapy is of relatively recent origin, this particular concept has deep and distant roots—it has precedents in Greek philosophy of the Stoic school, particularly that of Epictetus, who said two millennia ago: "People are disturbed not by things, but by their view of things."

To change a "view of things" that is causing pain and problems in a more realistic direction is the central goal of cognitive-behavioral therapy (CBT). Its strategies serve this goal by fostering awareness of the beliefs and thought patterns that we take for granted—challenging the natural assumption that the way things seem to us is the way they inevitably are—leading us to examine such patterns closely and objectively, and in this way to gain the power to alter them. In so doing it aims to increase the capacity to cope with the demands and stresses of life.

Where psychodynamic therapy is often loosely structured and open-ended, CBT tends to be highly organized. The first sessions are generally devoted to taking a detailed history that includes current and past problems, family history, previous treatments, and medical conditions, and perhaps will involve formal questionnaires to measure the severity of anxiety and depression. The goal is a full understanding of the difficulties that have brought you to therapy and the first steps toward knowing what's going on behind them: the beliefs and thoughts that create and maintain anxiety, depression, anger, and inability to work effectively.

With the help of the therapist, you will probably formulate explicit goals for your therapy. These also will be put in concrete terms: "I want to be more productive at work"; "I want to be more social with people . . . to manage my household more effectively . . . to take better care of myself physically." You may then set priorities—which goals are most feasible to address first, and so forth—and agree on a *treatment plan* that will work toward these ends.

The plan will probably include an estimate of the duration. While a therapist usually doesn't establish a rigid timetable, the approach is "time-sensitive" and takes seriously the goal of working as quickly and efficiently as possible. Many problems are addressed in six to twelve sessions, but long-standing, pervasive difficulties may take a year or more. Sessions ordinarily start out weekly but may in time be spaced out to every other week, or even longer intervals as the work progresses.

Like the therapy as a whole, each session is structured. Instead of seeing what evolves through free association, there's an agenda, which might typically include going over what happened the week before, what problems may be coming up, and what will be discussed during the hour. Some therapists will suggest that you spend a few minutes before the session starts, perhaps even fill out a form, to focus on material of importance.

"But we try to remain flexible," says Judith S. Beck, Ph.D., director of the Beck Institute for Cognitive Therapy and Research in Bala Cynwyd, Pennsylvania. "If important things come up in the course of the session, we'll decide together whether to pursue the new topic."

Therapists take a more active role than in many other kinds of therapy but make an effort to ensure that this remains essentially a *collaborative* role. "We make decisions together," Dr. Beck says. "What problems to tackle, what solutions to try, what to discuss during the session." The therapist is likely to share her thoughts about whatever is revealed in therapy, and solicits feedback on what is and isn't working well.

The actual work that goes on in a session may focus on the specific thoughts that accompany problematic behavior and unpleasant feelings. According to cognitive theory, between an event and your reaction to it come your thoughts about it; your stream of "self-talk" creates the reality that arouses emotion and spurs you to action. At first, it may be difficult to become attuned to these thoughts, particularly the automatic ones that arise almost as a reflex, but it becomes easier with practice.

Toward this end, the therapist may encourage you to describe typical situations in which you have had difficulty, and to articulate the thoughts and identify the actions that accompanied them. What were you doing on a specific occasion when you became particularly depressed, when your temper flared up, when you felt insecure? What thoughts were running through your head?

Once you start listening to your own mind, the connections that emerge can be most revealing. There's a snafu at work and you feel extremely anxious. Why? If you're alert, you may find the feeling was preceded by thoughts like "I'll never get this right" and "Everyone will know how incompetent I really am," which lead to an imagined cascade of dire consequences up to and including the loss of your job. Your spouse is ten minutes late for lunch, and you start to feel down. Before the feeling came the thought: "She's always so inconsiderate . . . she really doesn't care about me."

The therapist may help you to identify logical distortions that repeatedly lead you to grief. Among them are *black-and-white thinking* (everything seems all good or all bad, with no middle ground), *catastrophizing* (worst-case scenarios spiral down from a simple setback to dreadful consequences), or *mind reading* (you assume malicious motives in others). Becoming aware of the irrational fallacies that you commit without thinking is the first step to correcting them.

CBT goes beyond distorted thoughts to the *belief systems* that underlie them. As you become aware of the patterns that repeat themselves in one situation after another, certain fundamental beliefs about yourself, the world and other people, and the future may emerge. Beliefs like "I'm defective and inadequate," "People are unreliable," "I'm unlovable," or "Nothing will work out the way I want it to" are common in depression, while "People are malicious" and "The world is a dangerous place" are often prominent in the worldview of angry people.

These belief systems or "schemata" act as lenses that emphasize some parts of your experience and keep you from seeing others. If "I must be perfect in everything I do" and "Everyone must approve of me" have become established in your mind as the "rules" that make sense of life, you're likely to dwell on events that confirm your view and discount those that don't.

The therapist may suggest that you put yourself in the role of a scientist, who makes objective observations and evaluates data to test the validity of her hypotheses. Propositions like "People are always unreliable" or "Nothing ever works out the way I want" can't stand up under close scrutiny, and once this becomes clear, you can start to develop more realistic, constructive alternatives.

While CBT is for the most part a therapy that focuses attention on the events and responses that make up life in the here and now, it may look backward to explore the origins of these beliefs. What circumstances of your childhood might have given you the idea that you were "unlovable"? What subsequent events maintained this idea? In this way CBT resembles psychodynamic therapy but still retains its focus on conscious material—what happened and what you thought—rather than deeper unconscious structures and processes.

The "behavior" part of cognitive-behavioral therapy also follows a scientific model, often taking the form of "experiments" to test your expectations and beliefs and to investigate new ways of living that may work better. People who are depressed, for example, tend to "shut down"—they engage in few activities and reduce or eliminate contact with others. Inertia keeps them in bed or in front of the TV. An initial part of the treatment plan, then, might emphasize planning and carrying out potentially pleasurable activities—*even though you don't feel like doing them.* The strategy might include predicting how much you'll enjoy going to a movie, then noting how much you actually enjoy it (the chances are it will exceed your expectations). Or to keep careful track of the thoughts that arise and keep you from having a good time.

This approach reverses the way much other therapy works (and the way most of us habitually run our lives), which is to focus attention on feelings and refrain from doing things until we're "in the mood" and ready to do them. It recognizes that behavior is easier to change than emotions, and that constructively modifying the first is likely to have a beneficial effect on the second; after you start going out, in other words, you may begin to feel in the mood to go out.

In general, what happens during the CBT session itself is only a small part of the therapy. "Homework" that takes the process out into the real world often plays a key role. Unlike the homework you had in school, these assignments aren't handed down from a higher authority but arrived at by a process of collaboration; you only do what you think you can do, and agree will be helpful.

Some assignments may be ongoing: keeping a journal, for example, to pinpoint the situations in which strong feelings of depression or stress arise, the thoughts that precede or accompany these feelings, and how you deal with them. A more focused task might be to engage in a certain number of friendly "small talk" exchanges with salespersons and others during the following week, or to call friends with whom you have been out of touch.

If you don't carry out an assignment, this isn't a failure but material to discuss in the next session. Was the task itself too vague or overwhelming, or did thoughts come up (e.g., "What's the use?") that blocked your carrying it through? This is similar to the way "resistance" is handled in psychodynamic therapy—potentially valuable grist for the mill.

The therapist may encourage you to take notes during the session, or to pause for the last five minutes to consider and jot down the things you think are important to remember, so you'll have them to refer to during the upcoming week. Readings in books or informational brochures about particular conditions like anxiety or obsessive-compulsive disorder are also frequently incorporated into the treatment plan. It's all part of the emphasis on learning that's at the heart of cognitive-behavioral therapy.

## What CBT Works For

CBT lends itself well to the kind of scientific testing that documents effectiveness: it can usually be applied in the six-to-twelve-week periods favored by clinical trials; it focuses on specific, measurable goals; and it uses specific strategies that can be described in formal manuals and applied consistently. In fact, these kinds of therapy have amassed impressive credentials, in terms of clinical study data.

The most compelling results have been in the treatment of depression and anxiety. A meta-analysis (a study that examines data from a number of separate research studies) of twenty-eight controlled trials found CBT to be better than no treatment or other kinds of therapy for major depression. And a number of studies suggest that it is as good as drug treatment (although some suggest that medication is more effective in particularly severe cases). When CBT is added to medication, people who have recovered from depression appear less likely to relapse.

CBT seems similarly useful against most types of anxiety disorder. For panic disorder, it has been shown to be nearly as effective as drug treatment in the short-term relief of symptoms, and more effective in the long term (chances of relapse are less after the treatment is withdrawn). The American Psychiatric Association specifically includes certain types of CBT in its *Practice Guideline for the Treatment of Panic Disorder.*

The most fully tested and apparently most effective psychotherapy for obsessive-compulsive disorder is a behavioral approach called *exposure and response prevention,* in which patients are exposed to the things they fear and prevented from performing the rituals that normally keep anxiety at bay. It's a demanding program, but when patients stay with it, they appear to do as well as those who take medication.

Exposure therapy and systematic desensitization are thus far the strongest strategies for treating post-traumatic stress disorder, and the treatment plan often involves a cognitive component as well.

The American Psychiatric Association's *Practice Guideline for the Treatment of Eating Disorders* notes that controlled studies have shown CBT and simple behavioral techniques (such as keeping a food diary) to be helpful for bulimia. A summary of ten controlled trials cited by the American Psychological Association found improvements in about three fourths of eating-disorder patients who were treated with CBT.

*Dialectical behavior therapy* (DBT), a method that adds some principles of Eastern meditation to the behavioral approach, has been shown by repeated controlled studies to be effective in the treatment of borderline personality disorder. In particular, it reduces self-destructive behavior in seriously ill individuals. Other research suggests that DBT can help in substance abuse and eating disorders.

As this summary should make clear, there are different kinds of CBT, and the strategies that work for depression may have little to offer someone with panic attacks. As ever, the bottom line is the therapist's expertise in treating you and your unique problems.

## Finding CBT

The Association for Advancement of Behavior Therapy [http://www.aabt.org/CLINICAL/CLINICAL.htm] maintains a referral service that lists members who practice various types of behavior and cognitive psychotherapy, organized geographically. The amount of detail for each therapist varies but may include training, specialties (e.g., the disorders they treat), and "practice philosophy" as well as basics like their degrees and contact information.

The Academy of Cognitive Therapy [http://academyofct.org/Links/CertifiedMembers.asp] can refer you to licensed therapists who practice a specific type of CBT, developed by Aaron Beck, that has deep theoretical and research foundations and has been used in many studies. Members of the organization have advanced training in cognitive therapy and have submitted tapes and transcripts of sessions, demonstrating their expertise.

*Rational-emotive behavior therapy* is one of the original forms of CBT, with a strong focus on dysfunctional thoughts and behaviors. About twelve thousand therapists have been trained in its application. Members of the Albert Ellis Institute (Ellis originated the approach) throughout the country are listed at http://www.rebt.org/refer.html.

# Chapter 7

—

# STRENGTH IN NUMBERS

*Group Therapy*

People have a natural tendency to form groups. The family and tribe and nation, the club, the gang, the corporation—groups are as diverse as the members who compose them and the purposes they serve. But they all seem to generate power that exceeds the sum of their parts.

Therapy groups are no exception. The idea of coming together with others for the explicit goal of insight and change is nearly as old as the idea of psychotherapy itself, but the original therapy group was actually convened for medical purposes. In 1906, physician Joseph Pratt gathered tuberculosis patients to encourage them in maintaining healthy lifestyle patterns (exercise, good food, fresh air) that promote recovery. His motive was educational, but Pratt noted that simple inclusion in the group brought unexpected benefits, instilling hope and fostering members' emotional well-being.

Today, proponents of nearly every form of psychotherapy endorse the value and vitality of the group approach. Psychodynamic therapists and behaviorists may differ substantially in their ideas of how the mind and personality operate, why things go wrong, and what therapeutic strategies can best make them right, but they agree that the work can often be done effectively and efficiently when patients do it together.

The logic may not be immediately evident. An arrangement where seven or ten people meet with a single therapist for ninety minutes sounds simply like a diluted form of the familiar one-on-one therapy situation in which you alone are the focus of professional attention and wisdom. And if each of those people has been motivated to enter therapy by difficulty, often acute, in dealing with his own problems, what can he offer you in dealing with yours?

## What Is a Therapy Group?

Just as psychotherapy is a unique form of relationship, a therapy group is a special kind of gathering. Like psychotherapy, it has an explicit purpose: insight and change. There may be other rewards—education, companionship, diversion—but these are all enlisted, ultimately, in the service of the therapeutic goal; there's no other reason for everyone to be there.

As the distinction between "therapy" and "counseling" may seem blurry at times, so is the border between therapy groups and such gatherings as "support" or "self-help" groups. These have an essentially more limited purpose—helping members cope with one kind of problem (say, a medical illness or a life situation like recent divorce). A self-help group has no leader, and a support group often has a professional whose role is largely to provide information and keep things focused on the organizing issue.

Helping members cope with problematic areas of their lives is a significant goal of most therapy groups as well, but sights are set higher: to achieve deeper, more lasting change and growth. And here, although emphasis differs from one orientation to another (just as it does in different kinds of individual therapy), a principal focus of attention is what happens in the group itself. The relationships you form with other members are a subject of discussion, a source of therapeutic effects, and perhaps the ultimate raison d'être of the group.

The fact that a therapy group has much in common with gatherings in the "real world" is a source of its strength. It has been compared to a "miniature society" and a microcosm of the family and community. In other words, people act the same way in therapy as they do out in the world.

Like individual therapy, though, the group offers a setting that is not available elsewhere: a *safe* place where you can be yourself without fear of alienating others or facing retribution. In fact, the candid disclosure of thoughts and feelings is actively encouraged in most groups as a condition of membership.

At work, among friends, even in the family, people are valued for their positive qualities and accomplishments; there's pressure, often far from subtle, to be cheerful, productive, competent. In a good therapy group, however, each member is appreciated for *who* she is: flaws and shortcomings, if expressed honestly and with a willingness to explore, can be as valuable as strengths. In most settings you must present yourself in a socially acceptable form; the group allows you to drop the mask.

Just being in such a social environment—feeling valued and accepted by peers you respect, without having to constantly prove your worth—can have a therapeutic effect, suggests David Hawkins, M.D., past president of the American Group Psychotherapy Association.

The same things happen in a therapy group that happen everywhere people come together: peer pressure develops, social influence molds, personalities mesh and clash, needs are repressed and expressed, met and frustrated. But here it's all fair game for exploration and insight.

"Most people who come for psychotherapy are struggling with interpersonal issues—they have major concerns in the areas of family, romantic, or work relationships," says Harold Bernard, Ph.D., president-elect of the American Group Psychotherapy Association.

"Working in an environment in which relationships get established and evolved, they have a firsthand opportunity to look at what might be getting in the way of interpersonal success."

The setting itself, a relatively unstructured give-and-take social situation with the same people, week after week, is in fact likely to stimulate, perhaps in a heightened form, the same conflicts that prompted you to seek help in the first place. While in individual therapy you may spend a good deal of time *talking about* your difficulties with others in the real world, in a group you *live* them.

But of course, you talk about them too. As in individual therapy, what develops in the room is largely a relationship that exists to be analyzed. What's more, you have the opportunity to try out new, potentially more satisfying ways of interacting with others.

## What Happens in Group?

The typical group goes on for ninety minutes, more or less, and meets weekly. Like individual therapy, it may be of limited duration, with an explicit focus (social anxiety, for example) and the same people present at the beginning, middle, and end. Or it can be open-ended both in scope and duration, and go on literally for decades, with a cast of characters who join and leave as their needs demand.

What actually happens in a particular group depends in part on the approach of the therapist who leads it; as in individual therapy, there are broad divisions and subtle variations within them, and many if not most groups integrate elements from diverse sources.

The *psychodynamic* or intrapersonal approach uses the group format to focus on the same issues that are central in psychodynamic therapy: the unconscious conflicts and defenses of each member. The therapist-leader is likely to be more actively involved than in individual therapy, but less so than in other groups. His role includes directing attention to the ways in which issues like transference and resistance manifest themselves in interaction between members of the group.

Transference—bringing into the present feelings that originated in early-life relationships—occurs in the group setting just as it does in individual therapy. In fact, the group situation promotes the rapid development of transference and makes it possible for different relationship patterns to develop with different fellow members.

By the same token, the on-the-spot interplay of members' personalities supplies a fertile situation for exploring defense mechanisms used to avoid experiencing painful or threatening emotions, such as denial and the projection of one's own motives and feelings onto others.

The *interpersonal* approach focuses on the interactions among group members and what these may show about each person's relationship problems in the real world. Less attention is paid to unconscious patterns beneath the surface of the group, and more to promoting growth, maximizing the impact of positive experiences, and encouraging imitation of role models.

*Action-centered* approaches include cognitive-behavioral ways of using the group experience. Exercises like role playing may be involved, and the leader, as well as other group members, is likely to be quite active in helping you become aware of how irrational thoughts and distortions are shaping your reactions. The group is a perfect setting for reality testing—to compare your fantasies of what others think about you and your behavior with what's actually going on.

As in individual cognitive-behavioral therapy, the group leader may explicitly act as a teacher, instructing the group about how events and situations trigger thoughts, which then generate emotions. He may assign homework, directing members to try out behaviors they habitually avoid (being more assertive, for example) or to keep track of their thoughts in real-life situations and report the results. The support of others who are engaged in the same enterprise helps strengthen each member in attempting tasks that she might find daunting or threatening.

What most groups, regardless of emphasis or ideology, have in common is an emphasis on *here-and-now* experience. The personal history of group members may come up, but it is usually in the context of events and interchanges that happen in the group itself. Even those groups that are based on the psychodynamic concept of the mind and personality are unlikely to delve deeply or at length into the past of any individual. In a similar way, participants often talk about situations in their current lives—relationship and work problems, for example—but these are connected to and illuminated by the interactions in the therapy room.

There may be only one mental health professional in the room, but most participants feel that much of the benefit comes from fellow members—a strength of virtually all groups is a kind of therapeutic synergy that arises from the combined contributions of diverse points of view.

In other words, you aren't "having therapy" only while you're talking about your problems, but also as you listen and react to others as they talk about theirs; surprising insights can arise when you see the relevance of other people's experience to your own; your life is illuminated from a new perspective. Simply recognizing that others share your problems lightens the burden of shame and isolation, and hearing how they deal with their difficulties can catalyze your own efforts.

Rewarding as group therapy may ultimately become, it's not often easy to get started. "Never, in all my years of doing this work, have I seen a person come into group therapy without being terrified," says James M. McMahon, Ph.D., a psychologist in New York City. A common fear is exposure—many of us harbor feelings of inadequacy and worthlessness and construct elaborate defenses to hide this vulnerability from others. We're afraid that we may be forced to reveal more about ourselves than we want to in the name of the "honesty" the group stands for.

"I assure them that a group is not a confessional," says Dr. Bernard. "You don't have to bear your soul before strangers, and it's up to you what you talk about and what you don't." In actuality, he says, fellow group members cease to be "strangers" very quickly, and most people soon and spontaneously feel inclined to talk about what's important to them.

The openness of the group and its liberation from the constraints of conventional courtesy constitute a source of considerable strength but also of anxiety—about the unconscious impulses, hostile and sexual, that may lurk beneath the surface. A good group leader manages to preserve the strength while taming the threat; his presence makes it possible for members to "check their guns at the door," says Dr. McMahon. Participants can allow themselves to express deep, powerful levels of feeling, and experience the similar feelings of others, in the safe space created by skillful supervision.

Like any kind of therapy, the group is bound by ethical and practical rules. While anything can be said candidly and forcefully, feelings are not to be acted upon. Regular attendance is especially important, because the integrity of the group itself is affected by the reliability of its members. Outside contact may be encouraged in certain groups, but for the most part it is frowned upon if not forbidden outright, or allowed only with explicit conditions (e.g., it must be reported to the rest of the group). And sexual contact between members is always taboo.

Confidentiality is a key and sometimes uneasy issue. The therapist, of course, is bound by the rules of his profession, but group members have no professional code of ethics to uphold. Everyone *agrees* not to talk about what happens within the confines of the room, and most especially not to mention fellow group members by name or by identifying detail. But there's no authority to enforce this stronger than the integrity of the individuals involved.

## What Group Works For

Therapists who work with groups tend to be enthusiastic about the range of people for whom they're helpful—just about anyone, it can be argued, will benefit from the experience of meeting regularly with peers in an atmosphere that encourages honesty and acceptance.

The most obvious benefits are for those whose relationship difficulties bring them to therapy. This embraces a wide area—work problems, intimacy issues, family strife, loneliness. Even diagnoses like anxiety or depression almost always include a substantial interpersonal component. The support of others and the insight that comes from groups may be useful in overcoming the isolation of depression, and anxiety eases when people become more comfortable being with others.

Many people in groups have individual therapy at the same time, often with the same therapist, and the two areas of effort, the deeper and the broader, complement each other. Or group may follow a period of individual therapy, to continue the work and take it further.

While many groups are heterogeneous—there's a mix of ages, genders, and problems—others are more targeted, gathering people who have life situations in common and share the same difficulties. Each approach has its strength. Specialized groups are quicker to bond and develop the group spirit that makes it possible to work together. But many therapists think that these groups tend to remain fixated on the problems that members share, and are less likely than diverse groups to explore personal and interpersonal issues.

As in individual therapy, how much any group can accomplish depends to an extent on how long it lasts. Short-term groups (those that meet for several months, usually with a fairly definite agenda) can effectively address immediate problems and disorders such as anxiety. But those that last for years carry the potential to achieve deeper, more lasting changes.

The group setting has some obvious practical advantages. One trained therapist can work with a number of people at once, and the cost to each is lower (about half of what it is in individual therapy). But ample documentation shows that it isn't simply a cut-rate, second-best version of the real thing. In fact, studies that have analyzed and compared the results of literally hundreds of different studies have found group therapy to be as effective as (and in some cases more effective than) individual therapy.

In particular, there is convincing scientific evidence that group cognitive-behavioral therapy works well for social phobia, according to the American Psychological Association. This should not be overly surprising, in that this disorder, which involves anxiety over relating to and being judged by other people, seems to need exactly what the group has to offer: the opportunity to work through and become desensitized to that fear in a safe environment. It is especially encouraging that, in several studies, patients maintained their gains for years, after treatment that lasted no more than twelve sessions.

Groups of diverse kinds are considered by many psychiatrists to be "the preferred mode of psychotherapeutic treatment" for people with problems related to alcohol or drug use, according to the American Psychiatric Association's *Practice Guideline for the Treatment of Patients with Substance Use Disorders.*

The APA's guidelines for panic disorder note that several studies have found cognitive-behavioral therapy to work as well in group as it does one-on-one, while its guidelines for depression note that the group approach for this disorder is supported by "clinical experience rather than systematic controlled studies." A group may be particularly useful when depression develops in connection with bereavement or chronic illness.

A particularly striking example of the power of the group was provided in a classic study, conducted at Stanford University, of a "supportive-expressive" therapy group for women with metastic breast cancer. This went beyond the standard support group that brings together people with severe illness, in that it was led by a trained professional and encouraged deeper exploration of anxieties about the disease, fear of death, and other painful issues.

At follow-up years later, it was found that women who had participated in the therapy groups lived an average of eighteen months longer—double the survival time—than women who had not had the therapy.

## How to Find a Group

Many people become involved in group therapy when it is suggested by the therapist they're seeing for individual treatment. The advantage here is that the therapist knows you well, can place you in a group whose composition is well suited to your needs, and is in a good position to explain the group and the rationale of the treatment to you.

If you are seeking group therapy on your own, the American Group Psychotherapy Association has a referral service [www.agpa .org, or call toll-free 877-668-2472], which includes a list of its members and the registry of Certified Group Psychotherapists. Both AGPA members and Certified Group Psychotherapists are mental health professionals who have special training and experience in leading groups.

As when seeking any kind of therapy, it's best to meet and interview several therapists and choose one with whom you are comfortable and who you feel can be of help. Before you start with any group, make sure the leader takes time to explain in detail how the group works, tell you what to expect, and answer your questions. Research has confirmed that people do much better in group if they are knowledgeable and well prepared.

## Chapter 8

—

# CLOSE TO HOME

## Family Therapy

Psychotherapy has never ignored family ties. To a psychoanalyst, early family life gives an indelible imprint to the personality. How the family drama of the first years is played out can mean anxiety, depression, neurosis, or fulfillment later on; the key characters among whom we are cast largely determine how we see ourselves and others for the rest of our lives.

Like so many other developments in psychotherapy, the basic idea of *family therapy* owes a great deal, in its origins, to this kind of psychodynamic thinking. What made it different was the influence of a concept that developed during the 1940s in the hard sciences: *systems theory*. The key insight here is that you simply can't understand an element (an atom, a cell, a human being) except in its context—the system of which it is a part.

The clearest example (and an original focus of interest for systems theory) is the living organism. The human body is composed of cells, but the life of a single cell is inconceivable without its connections to other cells, the exchange of chemicals, ions, hormones, and enzymes that enable it to function. Cells are grouped into organs, each capable of nothing except as part of a vast system that supplies it with blood, oxygen, and nutrients, and receives whatever it manufactures.

In a healthy body, not only does each organ play a role, it is in turn supported by the whole. If a body isn't functioning well, its parts are going to suffer—some, perhaps, more obviously than others.

A healthy body isn't static but can flexibly adapt to its environment and the passage of time. There are strong forces that maintain stability (that keep your body temperature normal whether you go into a hot or cold place, for example), but this steady state can also evolve in an orderly manner that allows all its parts to function properly in the midst of change.

While other kinds of therapy pay attention to the individual's past and present family relationships, in family therapy these relationships are absolutely central. This represents what scientists call a "paradigm shift": from a concentration on the individual to a focus on the system in which he has developed and in which he lives.

Phoebe Prosky, M.S.W., family therapist and director of A Center for the Awareness of Pattern in Freeport, Maine, calls this "ecological thinking" and compares it to the way the natural environment is understood as an interconnected network of parts in constant and dynamic interaction. "In family therapy, it isn't the individual who is in treatment. The person with the 'problem' is like the valve on top of a pressure cooker; the problem is the manifestation of a larger pattern."

This is not to say that family therapists deny the existence of factors specific to the individual—biological disturbances, for example, that can play a key role in mood disorders. But if an adult is depressed or anxious, or a child behaves badly in school—there is, in other words, what seems like a highly personal problem—her relationships within her family most likely have a strong effect on maintaining it. And attempts to deal with the problem must include changing the way the family functions.

## What Is a Family?

The term "dysfunctional family" has become something of a glib if not frivolous element in the contemporary lexicon. But in family therapy its meaning is quite specific. When functioning properly, a family not only meets its own needs as a unit (it stays together, everyone has enough to eat, a place to sleep, etc.) but also nurtures each member's ability to live a satisfying life.

A well-functioning family is a system in equilibrium. Its members are connected in a way that allows mutual support while fostering independence and growth. The *boundaries* between individuals are distinct but permeable; like a cell membrane, they keep each separate but allow the back-and-forth flow of emotions and affections among them.

Each family has its own culture, a set of rules or principles that enable it to go through daily life smoothly ("Don't interrupt while your mother is talking" or "You can joke with your little sister, but don't go too far."). Each of us has multiple roles, ways of behaving appropriate to our place in the family. Much that happens in the family follows well-established patterns of interaction, in which roles mesh as in a performance by a skillful and experienced ensemble of actors.

A healthy family is neither rigid nor chaotic. It can change when the occasion warrants it. The needs and desires of members may come into conflict: a healthy family can balance them. It's when the network of connections, interactions, and relationships that make up the family system fail to serve the needs of its members that it becomes dysfunctional.

From this point of view, if a person comes (or is brought in) for help, he is regarded as the "identified patient" or "identified client." The symptoms that are causing distress to himself and others show that there's something wrong not just with him but with the family of which he's a part; he expresses the whole family's dysfunction (some therapists call him the "symptom bearer" for the family).

Why him? As the way the family functions unfolds and is better understood, it may become clear that his behavior represents an attempt to maintain the family's stability; it perhaps reflects a desire, however unfortunate, to help others and keep the family together. Or it may simply be that he is particularly vulnerable to the stresses that affect the family.

This shift of emphasis has one immediate and positive effect: it relieves the identified patient of the shame and blame that often falls on the person with problems. If the whole family is involved in the difficulty, everybody shares responsibility for trying to set things right.

Understandably, this new perspective may not be welcomed by all family members. It's far more comfortable to say "Poor Jim, he sure needs help" or "I suppose he needs help, but does he have to be so impossible?" than it is to say "We have a problem." The "art" of family therapy often involves showing that it is in everyone's interest to look at things realistically and to do the work this perspective demands.

## Who Goes for Family Therapy?

Most often, family therapy is sought by couples in conflict or who are considering separation or divorce ("marital therapy" may be considered a distinct form of therapy or an application of the family approach) or when children who are living at home have behavior problems or otherwise cause distress to their parents. But adult siblings who want to get along better may benefit, as may adult children whose relationship with a parent is problematic. The formation of "blended families" through divorce and remarriage has created complex and often troubled systems that may involve interlocking sets of parents and semisiblings.

The standard image of family therapy, where the therapist meets with a number of family members at once, is one common arrangement: parents and children, and at times grandparents and other relatives too, have joint, usually weekly sessions. But the cast of characters may fluctuate from one session to the next, and some family members may opt out altogether. In such cases the therapist will work with those who do come, with the idea that they will influence the others through a kind of "domino effect" on behavior.

It is even possible to use this approach with an individual: Murray Bowen, one of the pioneers of the field, often worked with just one family member, sending her back to try to change family patterns. "Family therapy has nothing to do with the number of people who are in the room," says Phoebe Prosky. Its hallmark is the particular way that the therapist thinks about problems—as glitches in a system—and how this generates strategies for treatment.

A key feature of this approach is how it redefines the presenting problem. To understand a difficult relationship between a mother and her adolescent daughter, the therapist is likely to ask who else lives in their home. Where is the father? Even if he is hundreds of miles away, the girl's relationship with him may be a key to the trouble. Are the grandparents involved in their lives? Finding out as much as possible about other family members makes clearer what *world* the difficulties arose in, and what changes may be helpful.

One family came in to see a family therapist in Pennsylvania because its two adolescent children, a boy and a girl, were missing school and suffering from headaches and other stress symptoms. The father had remarried, it turned out, and the children's mother and stepmother were in constant conflict. After five sessions that brought the two women together, the teenagers' problems largely resolved.

## What Happens in Family Therapy?

There's no single school of family therapy, any more than there is one approach to individual psychotherapy. In a similar way, while many therapists have a basic orientation that relies heavily on one theory, most are eclectic, letting their experience shape the way they work and drawing from diverse sources in choosing what's most effective for each situation.

For the most part, family therapy is of limited duration: ten to twenty weekly visits is typical. Sessions may be the usual "therapeutic hour" of forty-five to fifty minutes or may last longer, particularly if a number of people participate.

While there are differences, depending in part on the personalities involved and the theoretical orientation, the family therapist is likely to play an active role in therapy; she will not sit by on the sidelines while the family thrashes things out. At the same time, as in group therapy, her role will probably be restrained and catalytic: not *doing* as much as facilitating the interactions of family members.

In particular, the family therapist must form a therapeutic alliance that is different from, and perhaps more nuanced than, that of an individual therapist. It means simultaneously developing an effective working relationship with several people at once, without taking sides, amid the contending forces and conflicted loyalties that make up family dynamics. He may occupy a role that is part concerned family member and part neutral outsider. It's a balancing act like that of the family itself.

Most kinds of family therapy have similar aims: to reduce distressing symptoms in individual members and resolve problems of the family itself; to increase members' intimacy and ability to tolerate their differences; to promote self-esteem, facilitate clear and effective communication, and help members develop more flexible and adaptable roles. The belief is that this kind of work will do more than foster more harmonious relationships within the family; by altering the fundamental model for personal connections in general, it can improve relationships in the outside world as well.

The way the therapist works toward these goals may enlist approaches derived from one or more schools of therapy.

*Psychodynamic* or *insight-oriented* family therapy focuses on some of the same issues as individual therapy derived from psychoanalysis: unconscious conflicts, defense mechanisms, and the internal models of the self and others that are formed early in life (translated, however, into the way these are played out interpersonally within the family). Among the techniques that belong to this approach are *clarification*—following up on what family members say to get more depth and detail about their reactions to past events, for example—and interpretation, in which the therapist makes links between current and past behavior, conscious aims, and unconscious motives.

For example, he may help families become aware of how the defense mechanism of *projection* is involved in problematic behavior. A chronically misbehaving child or delinquent teen may have assumed the role of "bad boy" in a disciplined, high-achieving family. Everyone bemoans his misdemeanors but may give subtle signals of amusement, toleration, even approval. In the course of therapy, it may become clear that one or both parents has projected the "wild" side of his or her personality—the part that was repressed but never entirely stifled—onto the child, and he has learned to live up to their expectations.

*Family-of-origin* therapy also relates the present to the past but takes a wider view, considering material from three or even four generations. A basic principle is that patterns of relationship, behavior, and beliefs are transmitted from one generation to the next. The therapist may gather information about several generations and summarize them in a "genogram," a kind of family tree that graphically portrays the relationships among members and chronologically relates events in the family's life.

One goal of this kind of therapy is to foster *self-differentiation:* achieving workable connections among family members that are neither aloof nor overly involved.

Therapists of all kinds may see trouble between marriage partners as projections of unresolved conflicts within the families where they grew up. But one who applies family-of-origin principles might encourage partners to resolve these conflicts directly with the individuals with whom they originally developed, rather than only working them out with the spouse. People are often counseled to overcome estrangement from their families of origin, even to make trips home to learn more about the forces from the past that affect their present lives, and work at putting long-standing issues to rest.

*Structural therapy* focuses on working arrangements within the family: alignments where certain members join together or work against each other in carrying out family activities. It tries to identify and modify *coalitions,* dysfunctional patterns in which two family members form an alliance against a third, and *triangulation,* in which each parent demands that a child become his or her ally against the other.

A structural therapist will often be quite active in setting up situations that will reveal family dynamics and in making suggestions to alter rigid or destructive patterns. (The role has been seen as "stage director of the family drama.") For example, she may try to create situations in which the family will act out, right there in the session, the same conflicts that cause problems in the outside world, then encourage members to experiment with new, alternate ways of responding.

The therapist takes an even more active role in *strategic therapy,* which directly attempts to correct family patterns that cause difficulty; it is explicitly a problem-solving approach that spurs families into action. From this approach comes the use of *directives,* which assign tasks to family members to be done outside therapy, so that they will experience firsthand how it feels to behave differently with one another. The therapist may exaggerate problems to bring them into focus—telling a mother who indirectly undermines her husband's authority with their son, for example, to give the boy a quarter each time he disobeys his father. Prescribing the symptom—such as telling a battling couple to argue twice a week for two hours—can have a paradoxically helpful effect by leading the family to see more clearly the pointlessness of their behavior, or even to give it up as an act of joint rebellion against outside interference.

The principles and strategies of *cognitive behavioral therapy* are increasingly used in the family setting. As in individual CBT, the goal is to identify dysfunctional thought patterns and beliefs—but here they are explored within the context of the family. The thoughts, emotions, and behavior of each family member are constantly interacting with those of the others, which can lead to cycles of conflict that are difficult to break.

Of particular importance, says Frank Dattilio, Ph.D., director of the Center for Integrative Psychotherapy in Allentown, Pennsylvania, are the beliefs that members have about their family, and about family life in general. In addition, each family holds *its* core beliefs, a synthesis of the assumptions and life experience of its separate members, which may promote harmony or generate turmoil.

A virtue of this approach is its clarity and rationality. As in other kinds of family therapy, the therapist pays a good deal of attention to rigid roles and relationships that lead to conflict and cause unhappiness to individual family members. But CBT offers a clear way for participants to understand just what is happening, and suggests concrete steps for change. These may include keeping track of the thoughts that come up in problem situations, and agreements to try out new kinds of behavior.

## Couples Therapy

Couples, married and otherwise, are family therapists' most frequent clients. Although there are some ways in which the couple can be distinguished from larger family groups, most basic concepts of therapy are the same: it's a system that's under treatment, not two individuals, and the aim is to create new experiences, new understanding, and new patterns of relationship.

An ongoing relationship is a dynamic thing, subject to changing forces and the ups and downs of its own life cycle; even a couple that is well matched and usually harmonious may go through tumultuous times, especially during periods of stress brought on by unemployment, illness, or retirement.

While many couples seek therapy to work out conflicts when they feel uncertain whether to stay together or to separate, some simply want to strengthen or deepen their relationship, or smooth the way through a crisis. In a world in which the conventions of courtship are ambiguous and the roles open to the sexes are fluid, unmarried couples may seek help in charting the course of a relationship that is stagnating at an impasse between commitment and parting.

Often a couple is in conflict about concrete, specific issues—money, household tasks, planning—and the therapist will try to clarify the underlying interactions that recur through varying guises. A common pattern, for example, involves a "pursuer" and a "distancer." One partner needs a certain amount of space and independence to feel comfortable, while the other needs reassurance. "The more one reaches out, the more the other runs away," says Fred Piercy, Ph.D., head of the Department of Human Development at Virginia Polytechnical Institute and State University. "If you look at just one person's problem, you miss both."

An approach in this situation might be to examine the vulnerable feelings behind each person's inflexible responses (perhaps by exploring experiences in their families of origin) and to increase the degree of empathy each feels for the other. Or to promote alternative behavior patterns that will interrupt the destructive cycle.

Much contemporary couples therapy applies cognitive and behavioral principles. The therapist may actively teach the couple to develop more effective communication skills: for example, to replace accusations like "You never care how my day went at the office—all you do when I walk in is talk about yourself" with "When you don't ask me about my day, I feel neglected." The approach often means changing behavior first, on the theory that thoughts and feelings will follow. A woman whose husband wants her to call him during the day will agree to do it at least once daily, and he will agree to do something she wants—meet her for lunch every week, and pay household bills more promptly.

Therapy may focus on the sexual part of the relationship. Difficulties in this area, such as erectile dysfunction or lack of arousal, often respond to behavioral interventions, including exercises to substitute attention to the pleasurable feelings of contact for an anxiety-producing concentration on performance. Or therapy may deal more with emotions and thoughts that inhibit desire, such as anger. It may be multidimensional, adding medical evaluation and treatment to the psychological approach.

In fact, one strength of family therapy in general is its willingness to combine with other treatments. It may be conducted at the same time as individual therapy for one or more family members, or along with medication for depression or other emotional disorders.

## What Family Therapy Works For

There is considerable evidence from controlled trials that family therapy is more effective than no therapy at all in a number of situations, and often the results are better than with individual therapy. When problems are severe, however, family therapy usually is not enough; it works best as part of a larger package that may include medication or individual therapy.

Much research has focused on disorders of childhood and adolescence. A behavioral-oriented kind of family therapy, *parent management training,* has been shown to achieve significant improvements in children with severe conduct problems. At least seven studies found that various kinds of family therapy reduce adolescent delinquency and undesirable behavior, compared with individual therapy or no therapy.

Marital therapy has been shown to reduce distress and conflict better than individual therapy or none at all, but less than half of the couples involved become completely free of symptoms. Some studies also suggest that marital therapy reduces the likelihood of divorce, at least in the short term.

The treatment of alcohol and drug abuse is generally complex, and family therapy alone is rarely the answer. Involving spouses and other family members has been shown to increase the rate at which alcoholics enter treatment. While the family approach appears to improve abstinence in the short term, over time it has not been shown to be superior to individual therapy. There are fewer studies of drug abuse, but these have had similar findings.

Family therapy appears to be helpful even in major mental illnesses. Schizophrenia almost always requires drug treatment, but the addition of psychotherapy can improve response and reduce the risk of relapse. Therapies that involve the family in communication and problem-solving training and offer crisis intervention have been shown to lower relapse rates significantly, compared with medication alone. Patients in these families also function better socially than others.

In depression, several studies have found that behavioral marital therapy is as effective as other well-tested approaches (cognitive-behavioral therapy or interpersonal therapy) for women in distressed marriages.

## Finding Family Therapy

The same general guidelines for finding a psychotherapist apply—a referral from someone knowledgeable about the field or a friend or acquaintance who has had a good experience with a particular practitioner is a good place to start.

Psychotherapists of all sorts (psychiatrists, social workers, psychologists, counselors) take on families and couples, but not all have a true "systems" orientation that understands each person in terms of the whole, rather than as individuals who happen to live together. Ask a prospective therapist about her treatment philosophy and goals, as well as her education and experience with families.

What does she mean by family therapy? Her beliefs about divorce, and about individual freedom versus the good of the family, are worthwhile subjects of discussion, Dr. Piercy suggests.

Some states (forty-one, at a recent count) license family thera-pists. If yours is one of them, find out what experience and educa-tion it requires. The American Association for Marriage and Family Therapy [www.therapistlocator.net] has a referral service, which in-cludes details about the training and practice of members who choose to be listed.

## Chapter 9

—

# BEING THERE

*Humanistic Therapy*

Psychodynamic and cognitive behavioral therapies may not be "scientific" in the sense of molecular biology or physics, but they share an emphasis on close observation and analysis; they systematically investigate the dysfunctions behind each patient's difficulty, and subscribe to diagnostic systems that imply an analogy with physical disease. The therapist has a menu of techniques to use in attempting to correct something that has gone wrong—that is, a "disorder."

There's a whole family of therapies, however, that operates from a very different premise: what brings people to seek help, their practitioners say, is not necessarily disorder or dysfunction but issues related to everyday life; not pathology but the individual's sense of his limitations—in vision, awareness, growth—and his desire for greater fulfillment.

These therapies don't see emotional problems as "sickness," and generally prefer the term *client* to *patient*. Their aim is not to cure from without but to stimulate and invigorate positive change from within—to help the client realize his fullest potential.

Where psychodynamic therapy focuses on unconscious forces, and behavioral therapies on what can be observed and quantified, humanistic therapies (sometimes called "existential-humanistic" or "humanistic-experiential") emphasize subjective experience.

Humanistic therapy came into being as a reaction to what some psychologists saw as serious limitations of existing therapies. It was a "third force" inspired by the belief that in refusing to see the world from the client's point of view, psychodynamic and behavioral therapies failed to recognize her intrinsic value as a person, and that in using conventional methods, therapists imposed their views on clients in ways that inhibited growth and damaged self-esteem.

Actually, humanistic approaches have their origins as far back as the early twentieth century, in the work of Alfred Adler, a psychoanalyst who collaborated with Freud but took a broader view that emphasized the power of creativity and the drive to accomplish life goals. They came into particular prominence in the liberated, experimental atmosphere of the 1960s and 1970s.

The lines of demarcation are much less obvious today, as psychodynamic and cognitive-behavioral therapies have come to accept many of the core values of the third force, paying more attention to the subjective side of experience, and recognizing that the therapist is never a purely detached observer or authority figure but a fellow human being with feelings and responses that play a role in the therapy process.

Contemporary humanistic therapy is something of a mixed bag, embracing approaches that start from diverse philosophies and may look quite different from one another in practice. Some (such as existential and person-centered therapy) at least outwardly resemble more traditional forms of talk therapy, while newer variations may involve elements of "bodywork," spirituality, and even ecological values.

What tends to distinguish them as a group is less a specific set of techniques or a model of the mind than a perspective on life and an idea of what it means to be human. All put an emphasis on the experience of therapy itself, rather than intellectual processes that go on within it. The client is not asked to introspect, to recapture memories from his past, or to identify thoughts as they arise, but to be fully "present" in the session itself, open to the whole range of his perceptions, emotions, and physical sensations. These therapies focus on the innate capacity for health, recognize the search for meaning as an essential human need, and are grounded in a value system in which freedom and creativity are highly prized.

As names like "existential" and "humanistic" suggest, the soil from which these therapies grow is philosophy—where "humanism" represents a worldview that stresses personal responsibility rather than the influence of divine or other external forces, as well as a distinctly human capacity to seek and find fulfillment. It puts a premium on autonomy and dignity, and on a life lived fully and passionately.

## Existential Therapy

This approach makes freedom a fundamental principle. While recognizing the limitations imposed by society and physical realities, existential therapy stresses that each person remains essentially free—to choose an attitude toward his circumstances, and to extract meaning from his life. Where other therapies may lead you to look toward the past to understand the source of your difficulties, existential therapy is oriented toward the future as the open space where you can evolve, engage, and make your life meaningful through your actions.

*Man's Search for Meaning* is the title of the classic text of *logotherapy,* an early version of existential therapy developed by Viennese psychiatrist Viktor Frankl. He proposed that "the will to meaning" is as fundamentally human as the will to pleasure, and that a great deal of suffering comes from failure to satisfy its demands. Without explicit rules and the sort of coherent belief system provided by traditional cultures of the past, many people today experience life as empty and without purpose. Attempts to fill the vacuum are responsible for depression, addiction, and aggression.

No one can *give* you a sense of meaning, but in logotherapy the therapist will actively guide and facilitate the search, in part through challenging questions (for example, "Can you see anything positive about this situation?") or by encouraging a kind of self-detachment that will empower you to see your fears and situation in a fresh perspective.

Beyond the need for meaning, existential therapy addresses the basic facts of the human condition: freedom, isolation, responsibility, the inevitability of death. It recognizes that a certain kind of anxiety isn't pathological, but inescapable in the face of these facts, and a consequence of exercising one's freedom.

What existential therapy tries to do is help clients to live honestly with the realities of existence, to break out of the restricted world they've created in attempting to cope with the natural anxieties of life, to exercise their freedom and autonomy and accept responsibility for their actions—to realize their potential for becoming more fully alive and recognize that they alone can choose how to use this vitality.

Toward these ends, the therapist may take an active role in challenging a client's assumption of "victimhood," and encourage him to confront when and how he is avoiding decisions—that is, avoiding freedom. Techniques are diverse and chosen for their usefulness, and may include some drawn from cognitive-behavioral therapy, such as desensitization or reframing the way you view a situation (e.g., as a challenge rather than a threat); and from psychodynamic therapy, such as free association. Directing attention to the details of experience as it is unfolding, the therapist calls upon the client to become more receptive to the sense of being alive.

The relationship between therapist and client is as central as it is in psychodynamic therapy, but not as a subject for analysis; rather, it stimulates and supports change. As critical as what the therapist *does* in the session is how she *is:* the goal is to be fully "present" as much as possible—involved, responsive, authentically herself. Not only does this provide a model of growth and self-realization, it creates an encouraging setting in which the client can face the anxieties that freedom and an unflinching look at the facts of life must arouse. The genuine, unguarded person-to-person relationship of therapy is an antidote to feelings of isolation and alienation.

There has been little systematic research into the effectiveness of existential therapy. It may be particularly helpful for people who are struggling with identity issues, such as at times of transition (aging, for example) and changes in life circumstances.

Detailed information about existential and similar therapies, including a list of people who practice them, can be found at the International Network on Personal Meaning, operated by the Graduate Program in Counseling Psychology of Trinity Western University [www.meaning.twu.ca].

## Person-Centered Therapy

The key premise of *person-centered* or *client-centered therapy* is faith in the innate capacity for positive growth and constructive change—an unwavering emphasis on what's right, rather than what needs to be fixed. Its goal is not relieving symptoms per se but promoting "self-actualization" or "self-realization." It aims to assist people in overcoming obstacles to growth and becoming all they're capable of being.

More rigorously than other therapies, it is *nondirective:* the therapist abdicates completely the role of authority, the one whose superior judgment or wisdom entitles her to solve the client's problems, correct his distortions, or set an agenda about the changes that need to be made. Autonomy should be respected in any kind of therapy; here it is the defining principle. "You are your own best therapist, the best expert about your own life," says Jerold Bozarth, Ph.D., of the University of Georgia.

Within each person is an "actualizing tendency"; like a plant seeking the light, at a deep, natural level you have the instinct to move constantly in a constructive direction, toward your highest potential. Emotional problems develop when this drive is stymied or deformed by circumstances (a parent who rigidly demanded that you conform to his standards, for example). But when the actualizing tendency is given the circumstances to flourish, you resolve your own problems.

So what is the therapist there for? Most important, to create the climate in which your natural tendencies for growth can operate, by establishing a relationship in which freedom and exploration are possible. "The therapist's only real job is to enter the world of the person empathically, and to convey complete trust," Dr. Bozarth says.

Toward this end, person-centered therapy puts a great deal of emphasis on the personal qualities and attitudes that the therapist brings to the relationship. She must be *genuine,* letting her behavior reflect what she experiences during the session, rather than trying to fill a predetermined role.

She needs to communicate to the client what Carl R. Rogers, the psychologist who developed the approach, called "unconditional positive regard," a kind of caring, acceptance, and respect that embraces the client as a person, regardless of his behavior. (This doesn't mean condoning the behavior itself, any more than a parent's love for a child means approving tantrums or bullying.)

Her attitude must be informed by *empathy,* a connection to the client's feelings that goes beyond abstract comprehension. It means not just understanding the other person's experience but sharing in it as if it were her own, without being lost in it. Empathy, in these terms, takes "seeing the world through the eyes of another" to a rich, human level.

According to the theory, simply to be in such a relationship over time (which also can occur in real life outside of therapy) has a highly positive effect. "It creates a safe atmosphere in which you can drop your defenses," Dr. Bozarth says. The therapist's attitude of complete honesty encourages you to be genuine in turn, to allow your behavior to match your feelings. The experience of being deeply valued and respected by the therapist enables you to accept *yourself* fully and unconditionally. The therapist's empathy promotes your ability to listen to your own feelings and to experience them in a more forthright way.

If you visit a person-centered therapist, he won't be applying "techniques" in the course of the session—out of the conviction that such an approach would depersonalize your relationship. He will, rather, be listening closely to you and encouraging you to express yourself. Questions will not be leading or probing but designed to confirm and facilitate his understanding of your feelings and point of view ("I think you're saying . . . am I right?").

While the effectiveness of person-centered therapy hasn't been subjected to controlled studies, it has shown itself to be comparable to that of cognitive-behavioral, psychodynamic, and other therapies. Proponents note that the therapist-patient relationship has repeatedly been found the most important determinant of success or failure, regardless of the specific method of therapy employed. And person-centered therapy puts the cultivation of this relationship at its center.

Articles, institutes, and other resources can be found at the website of Person-Centered International, a network organization dedicated to the promotion and application of person-centered principles [http://www.personcentered.com].

## Gestalt Therapy

Here the emphasis is on immediate experience, and the goal is insight. Where some other kinds of therapy value interpretation and understanding, gestalt encourages you to perceive, feel, and act outside the cloud of intellection. It takes the rejection of "shoulds" (important in certain kinds of cognitive-behavioral therapy) even further, making one of its key themes "What is, is."

Gestalt teaches how to use the internal and external senses fully, through exercises designed to focus awareness and open your eyes to a more spontaneous way of living. As in other humanistic approaches, an authentic, person-to-person relationship is a key element; the therapist must be "present" and empathic, in tune with his client's feelings as well as his own.

This kind of therapy devotes a good deal of attention to the physical aspects of experience. Therapists are alert to body language, particularly when it is at odds with what a client is saying, and are likely to direct clients' attention to the details of their perceptions and internal sensations.

Where another therapist might ask "Why," in gestalt the key questions are "What" and "How"—as in, "What are you feeling?" and "How are you making yourself angry?" This therapy aims not only to foster your awareness (of feelings or perceptions), but also to sharpen your sense of the process by which you become aware.

One of the central ideas of gestalt therapy is that anxiety, depression, and other emotional difficulties develop when individuals reject or disown parts of themselves, their ideas, their emotions, and their experience. Its goal is to help you to accept yourself fully by *integrating* what you had previously cast off.

Gestalt therapy doesn't ignore material from the past but regards it as alive in the present, as part of the here-and-now experience. Instead of talking *about* an encounter, person, or situation, you will be encouraged to become aware of how it *lives* in you, through fantasy or in the form of exercises, right there in the session.

Such exercises, or "experiments," are a distinctive feature of gestalt therapy. Questions like "What are you feeling right now?" or "What are you aware of as you talk?" might be asked in the course of cognitive-behavioral, psychodynamic, or other humanistic therapies. But exercises with their origins in gestalt (many of which have been appropriated by other therapies) are often dramatic and active, using guided fantasy and staged situations to explore feelings and thoughts in the here and now.

If a person comes into therapy and describes an encounter with a friend or family member the day before that left her angry and frustrated, she might be encouraged to visualize the situation, to imagine herself back in it, and describe what she is feeling and thinking as it unfolds.

Perhaps the most familiar is the "empty chair" technique, in which you imagine that a chair opposite you is occupied by a figure about whom you have strong feelings, or by a part of yourself. You address the chair, expressing your feelings, then reverse roles and take the other side, imagining and performing what that figure, or that part of yourself, would feel and say.

An exercise may take the form of exaggeration: you amplify a feeling or thought in order to feel it more intensely.

Dreams are often important in gestalt therapy, as they are in psychoanalysis. But instead of being interpreted, they are relived. According to the theory behind the method, every person and object in the dream represents an aspect of the dreamer. By acting out different characters in the dream and engaging in a dialogue between them, you can become more fully and vividly aware of various sides of yourself.

Gestalt therapy lends itself well to the group setting. Traditionally, it has been used for individuals whose inhibitions and self-imposed restrictions lie behind the various forms of anxiety and depression. Proponents say that it can be useful also for mind-body disorders (such as chronic digestive symptoms and problems related to muscle tension) and more severe conditions, including psychosis.

Its efficacy has not been tested under controlled conditions, but in a review of seven studies comparing therapy that uses gestalt-type approaches to cognitive or behavioral treatments, it came out slightly better.

—

For more information on gestalt therapy, including a directory of therapists, visit The Gestalt Therapy Page, a joint project sponsored by *The Gestalt Journal* and the International Gestalt Therapy Association [www.gestalt.org].

## Chapter 10

—

# MIND MEETS BRAIN

*Pharmacotherapy*

If you were to sum up in a word the way mental health care has changed in the last half century, that word would probably be *medication.* Forty years ago most psychiatry departments were headed by psychoanalysts, and residents spent much of their time learning psychotherapy; today biological psychiatrists rule, and questions like "Is there a future for psychotherapy?" appear regularly on the agenda at professional meetings.

To go by the evidence of popular media, the revolution is over, and drugs have won. Prozac, Ritalin, and their chemical cousins have been cover-story celebrities in *Time, Newsweek,* and *U.S. News & World Report,* and the newest antidepressant is regularly featured on the evening news.

Call it the combined power of science, the zeitgeist, and cold cash. Unquestionably, advances in our understanding of the brain and the biological basis of behavior, particularly in the last two decades, rival those in any other area of medicine. So much so that the 1990s were officially declared, by an act of Congress, "the Decade of the Brain" (the first organ to be accorded this honor).

Today, we have a whole arsenal of psychiatric medications that really work.

And as many social observers have noted, modern America seems to have a high affinity for drugs. If we so readily ease our bodily aches with a pill, why not medicate our blues away? It's in harmony with the contemporary tempo; swallowing a little green capsule each morning is easier to fit into a crowded schedule than visiting a therapist every week, and the results are visible a lot sooner.

On a less abstract plane, there's money to be made in meds. The multibillion-dollar pharmaceutical industry bankrolls psychiatric newspapers, hosts lavish seminars at professional meetings, and even pitches its wares direct to you on TV. On the demand side, accountants at the insurers and managed care companies who pay for most of our health care are impressed by the fact that an occasional stop at the doctor's for medication management seems more cost-effective than regular sessions with a clinical psychologist.

Of course, psychotherapy is not dead, nor is it asleep. Among mental health professionals, psychiatrists are still the only ones allowed by law to prescribe, and hundreds of thousands of psychologists, social workers, and others still ply their trade, without benefit of the prescription pad.

But something about psychiatric medication sends a lot of people to the barricades. On one side are the fully converted, who all but proclaim that psychotherapy is a disgraceful sham that keeps countless unfortunates from getting the medication they need. On the other are those who maintain with equal passion that drugs are toxic, period; when they're not actively destroying our bodies, they deprive us of the opportunity to grow through our suffering.

Realistically, pharmacotherapy, also known as psychopharmacology, is just one option for treating emotional problems. The most effective antidepressant, antianxiety, or antipsychotic drug in the world is sometimes a lifesaver, sometimes a reasonable choice, sometimes questionable, and sometimes ill-advised. And often pharmacotherapy is part of a treatment plan that includes other kinds of therapy as well.

## Biological Psychiatry

Where a psychoanalyst looks at a psychological disorder and sees unconscious conflict, and a cognitive therapist sees dysfunctional thoughts and beliefs, a psychopharmacologist is likely to see jumbled neurotransmitters and poorly regulated neural circuits. The problem lies not in our minds but in our brains.

This is an issue that has roots far back in history, and branches in disciplines that have little to do with mental health. The physicians of ancient Greece knew nothing about neurotransmitters, but they did explain mental troubles in terms of bodily fluids ("humors") that had gotten out of balance. Where they saw an excess of "black bile" as the cause of depression, we see a deficit of serotonin. The nature of the mind and its connections to the physical body, including the brain, has long been a staple of philosophical inquiry.

Psychiatry itself has been "biological" to some degree ever since its beginnings in eighteenth-century neurology, which sought an explanation for mental illness in abnormalities of brain blood vessels and in "irritable" nerve fibers. The influence of heredity—an extremely active area of modern research—was noted long before anyone suspected the existence of genes. That identifiable areas of the brain are involved in specific mental activities was established by the nineteenth-century French surgeon Paul Broca, who located the region responsible for speech.

Thanks to space-age technology, neuroscientists can now fashion images, in some cases down to the millimeter, of the brain regions involved in rational thought, decision making, impulse control, emotion, and memory, and delineate the circuits activated as we think, feel, and act. Their data are bringing into sharper relief the ways that malfunctions in neural wiring may be responsible for such troubles as panic, schizophrenia, and obsessive-compulsive disorder.

The reality behind the popular notion of mental illness as a "chemical imbalance" is an intricate system, still far from fully understood, of substances called neurotransmitters that are the life-blood of communication between brain cells and thus of mental activity. The first neurotransmitter, acetylcholine, was identified in 1926; today it is known that more than one hundred different chemicals carry signals among neurons. And knowledge of how they work has become increasingly refined, as more is learned about the sites on the nerve cell membrane ("receptors") that receive neurotransmitters, and the ways they regulate themselves and interact with one another.

For all the science that has burgeoned since, the first modern psychotropic drug (medication used to treat mental illness) was discovered by accident—and by a surgeon, not a psychiatrist. That was the antipsychotic chlorpromazine (Thorazine), whose calming properties were observed when it was used as an anesthetic aid, and which was given to psychotic patients for the first time in 1952. Around the same time, the first antidepressant, imipramine (Tofranil), was stumbled onto by researchers who were looking for a sedative.

The rest is history—a history of geometrically expanding research, development, and marketing that has led to dozens of antidepressants alone, along with whole families of drugs to combat psychosis, anxiety, and virtually every other disorder identified by psychiatry.

## Drugs or Therapy?

Only psychiatrists are licensed to prescribe drugs, but any mental health professional should know when they are indicated, and have an open-minded willingness to refer. Sometimes this is quite clear: almost anyone with a serious illness like schizophrenia or bipolar disorder (manic depression) should be on medication, whether or not they have therapy too. Depression serious enough to require hospitalization or that carries a significant risk of suicide is rarely treated with therapy alone.

But for many emotional problems the question "Psychotherapy or pharmacotherapy?" is a legitimate one. For most mood disorders, anxiety problems, and distressing behavior like anger outbursts and compulsive gambling, both drugs and therapy have arguments in their favor, and evidence of their effectiveness.

Among the factors a therapist may consider in deciding whether to recommend medication is the distress that the condition is causing. In the long run, psychotherapy may be as effective as drugs for panic disorder or moderate depression, but it takes longer to kick in. If your problems make it difficult to work or otherwise conduct your life, or cause you more pain than you are prepared to tolerate, the faster (although rarely immediate) effect of drugs may make them a more attractive choice.

Ultimately, however, *you are the one to decide,* and this may come down to a matter of values, beliefs, and worldview. Some people have strong positive feelings about the power of medicine and derive a sense of security from having the resources of modern science on their side. If you envision your problems as essentially biological in nature, you may feel that medication is the way to get at the root of what's gone wrong and correct it. You may find it simply more congenial to take a capsule than to talk about yourself in detail and initiate the kind of relationship that real therapy demands.

On the other hand, if you are the kind of person who prefers bearing a bit of pain to taking an aspirin and will run through a full course of natural remedies before going to the doctor, you probably won't want an antidepressant, either. The possibility of becoming reliant on a chemical for your well-being or of encountering side effects may be threatening. You may like the idea of working through your problems, and feel that understanding them in the framework of thoughts, feelings, and personal history will be more rewarding than simply taking something to relieve the symptoms.

These feelings are not to be ignored. For one thing, they can significantly affect the chances of success with whatever treatment you get; if you strongly believe in a medication, it's more likely to work, as evidenced by the placebo effect of inert substances that can bring remarkable improvements, even in physical ailments. On the other hand, if you accept a prescription because it's easier than arguing with your doctor, despite misgivings that you're taking poison into your system, the odds are that you'll take it erratically and stop sooner.

Because feelings about medication, pro and con, can be based on misconceptions and misunderstandings, it's best to talk about these feelings—as you would about anything else—with the therapist who recommends drugs or the psychiatrist who is prescribing them. Reluctance can reflect what some psychiatrists call "pharmacological Calvinism," a deeply rooted but not entirely rational belief that medication is "too easy" a solution and that relief must be earned by hard work. Questions like "How is medicating depression different from taking drugs for a chronic disease like high blood pressure?" can be productive to explore.

Rather than choosing between drugs and therapy, the best option may be both. The idea that the two can't mix—that medication interferes with the effect of therapy by undercutting motivation or interfering with the therapeutic relationship, for example—is dying out. By addressing the acute symptoms of depression, for example, medication can clarify thinking and make talk therapy more effective. Combined treatment has even become acceptable in psychoanalysis (psychotherapy, one might argue, in its purest form); in one study, one third of patients treated at a psychoanalytic institute were also given drugs.

At the same time, therapy improves the odds that medication will be taken responsibly, and can address problems that have developed as a result of long-standing illness (in personal relationships, work, self-image) and will remain even when symptoms of the disorder itself are successfully treated. For this reason, even people with conditions that absolutely require drugs, like schizophrenia, often have much to gain from concurrent therapy.

Convincing evidence of the value of combined drugs and therapy was provided recently by a large study reported in the *New England Journal of Medicine*. It divided more than six hundred people with chronic depression—it had lasted for years and resisted earlier treatment—into groups that were given an antidepressant, a sixteen-week course of cognitive-behavioral therapy, or both. Almost half of those who received the drug or therapy alone showed significant improvement, compared with nearly three quarters of those who had them together. Twice as many patients in the combined group made complete recoveries as in either single-treatment group.

Combined treatment has some practical drawbacks—expense, for one thing—and may not be necessary for everyone. An approach that many experts now endorse is starting with one or the other and keeping the second in reserve if the first proves inadequate alone.

## The Process of Pharmacotherapy

If you bring your problems to a psychiatrist, she will be the one to decide whether drugs are indicated, but if you're under the care of a psychologist or social worker, it will mean a referral to someone with the ability to prescribe. Many prescriptions for psychotropic medications—nearly half of those for antidepressants, for example—are actually written by primary care physicians, like internists and family practitioners.

There is nothing necessarily wrong with being in psychotherapy with one person and getting medication from another. (If a managed care company is paying for your treatment, it may insist on this arrangement.) But under these circumstances, it is highly advisable that the two work cooperatively and consult regularly. It is poor practice (and questionable ethics) for a therapist to arrange to have a physician write a prescription for you, sight unseen.

While many internists and family physicians have the know-how to treat uncomplicated depression and anxiety successfully, they are not the option of choice. Studies have repeatedly shown that nonpsychiatric physicians are more likely than specialists to misdiagnose emotional problems, to choose less-than-optimal medications, and to prescribe them in doses too low, or for periods too brief to be effective. And they generally spend far less time with each patient than a psychiatrist would—ten minutes compared with thirty for the average follow-up visit, in one survey.

The time factor is not trivial. Psychotropic medication should be prescribed on the basis of a full initial evaluation, which cannot be done in much under an hour. Among other things, you should have the opportunity to describe your emotional difficulties in detail, outline at least the most significant points of your personal history, and relate the treatment you have received thus far. The psychiatrist should know about your medical problems, if any, and whatever other drugs you are taking, prescription or over-the-counter, to minimize the risk of dangerous or unpleasant interactions.

When drugs are in the offing, you should feel free to ask for whatever information you need to decide whether or not to go forward: how they supposedly work, what treatment alternatives there may be, what makes the psychiatrist feel that this drug is needed for this problem. As with any medical or emotional condition, a second opinion is never a bad idea if doubts remain—about the therapy or the doctor.

*Side effects* are an issue with virtually all drugs, prescription and over-the-counter; the same chemical power that makes a medication effective can also have consequences that range from the inconvenient (increased appetite, digestive upset) to the troublesome (fatigue, nervousness, insomnia, loss of libido), to the frightening (seizures or bleeding). Some doctors are reluctant to volunteer this information, lest they frighten patients unduly. But with medical intelligence so widely available (on the Internet and elsewhere), this policy seems misguided, on practical as well as ethical grounds. At the very least, a psychiatrist (or any other physician) should tell you which adverse effects are common, and how long they are likely to last.

When you're taking medication, you should see the psychiatrist regularly, for visits that are more than a cursory ten-minute "med check." The effectiveness of pharmacotherapy, like psychotherapy, depends in large part on your relationship with the doctor. You should feel comfortable reporting not only on your emotional state and ability to function but also whatever difficulties you're having with the medication, and your feelings about taking it. You should be able to call him between visits if problems come up. The best medicine in the world won't work if it's not taken.

"Poor adherence to the prescribed treatment is a major reason why people don't get better," says Allan Tasman, M.D., chair of the Department of Psychiatry and Behavioral Sciences at the University of Louisville. "A number of studies have shown that about one half of prescriptions are not filled, or not taken properly."

When a medication is causing distress or doesn't seem to be working, too many people simply fiddle with the dose or stop taking it on their own. This is a poor idea for a number of reasons—for one, many psychotropic drugs can cause acute physical and emotional distress if stopped abruptly, and so should be tapered off gradually and under professional supervision.

If you don't feel comfortable airing your concerns, or if you feel they aren't being handled sensitively, you may need to change doctors.

## What Drugs Are Good For

Pharmacotherapy is more tightly regulated than psychotherapy. A therapist can do pretty much whatever she wants and call it therapy, as long as it seems credible to her patients and doesn't violate professional ethics or the law. But a drug must be approved by the federal Food and Drug Administration as safe and effective—an evidence-gathering process that typically involves years and literally millions of dollars' worth of research—before it can be prescribed.

Once a drug is approved for any indication, however, a licensed physician can prescribe it for whatever she wishes. If you're given Paxil (paroxetine) by a psychiatrist who is helping you control anger outbursts, you may think it has been FDA-approved for this purpose. But you'd be wrong. The drug has in fact been tested and FDA-approved for depression and certain anxiety disorders, but the doctor is prescribing it here on the basis of more limited data and her clinical judgment.

In general, don't take labels too literally. Psychotropics are classified as antidepressants, antipsychotics, and anxiolytics, etc., on the basis of their original indication, but they are widely prescribed for other purposes as well. There's nothing intrinsically wrong with this "off label" use; if prescriptions were limited to FDA-approved indications, the arsenal of useful treatments for anxiety disorders, mood disorders, eating disorders, and personality disorders would be much smaller. You might, however, want to ask your doctor about her rationale for prescribing what she does.

*Antidepressants* have become the most widely prescribed psychotropics, recently passing the previous leaders, antianxiety drugs like Valium. According to a study by the American Psychiatric Association, their use doubled in the decade after 1986.

The bulk of these prescriptions are for the new generation of such drugs: *selective serotonin reuptake inhibitors* (SSRIs). When Prozac, the first of these, was approved for use in 1991, it was hailed as a wonder drug. Now there are four others: Zoloft (sertraline), Paxil (paroxetine), Luvox (fluvoxamine), and Celexa (citalopram). They all work much the same way: by increasing the amount of the neurotransmitter serotonin available for communication between brain cells. (Too little serotonin, to simplify greatly, is believed to be a major mechanism in depression.)

What makes SSRIs special isn't so much what they do—like older drugs, each relieves depression in about two thirds of the people for whom its prescribed—as what they don't do. *Tricyclic antidepressants* like Tofranil (imipramine) and Elavil (amitriptyline) come with a laundry list of side effects including dry mouth, constipation, sexual difficulties, fainting, weight gain, and sedation. Serious heart problems are possible, if uncommon, and overdoses can be fatal. *Monoaminine oxidase inhibitors,* such as Nardil (phenelzine) and Parnate (tranylcypromine), are extremely effective drugs, particularly for certain kinds of depression. But they require dietary restrictions that make them risky: eating the wrong kind of cheese, for example, can make blood pressure soar.

Side effects with SSRIs are generally more manageable: digestive upset, headache, nervousness, and the like frequently disappear within weeks, and many patients are delighted to find that they lose, rather than gain, weight.

In the years since their arrival, however, it has become evident that these drugs aren't nearly as trouble-free as they first appeared. They take a toll on sexuality: up to 60 percent of patients suffer lost libido, erectile difficulties, or the like. After a year or so of treatment, most gain back the weight they lost, and a substantial minority gain some more.

More recently, SSRIs have been joined by newer drugs that affect other neureotransmitters in addition to serotonin: Wellbutrin (bupropion), Effexor (venlafaxine), Serzone (nefazodone), and Remeron (mirtazapine). They are comparably effective but have different side-effect profiles. (Serzone has little effect on sex, for example, but may cause extreme sedation in some people.) Everyone reacts differently; the wider menu makes possible a better fit between the drug and the individual.

The new antidepressants aren't just for depression. Certain of them have also been approved for panic disorder, obsessive-compulsive disorder, post-traumatic stress disorder, generalized anxiety, social phobia, bulimia, premenstrual syndrome, and smoking cessation. They have been used effectively in the treatment of personality disorders, impulse disorders (such as compulsive gambling), and problems as diverse as hypochondria and substance abuse.

Antidepressants are often started at a low dose, which is gradually increased as long as side effects aren't a problem. They take time to work, as much as four to six weeks to reach full effect. You may experience some improvement within a week or two, however.

The use of *anxiolytic drugs* (antianxiety drugs, a.k.a. minor tranquilizers), like Valium (diazepam) and Xanax (alprazolam), has fallen off somewhat in recent years, in large part because SSRIs are being prescribed in their place (for anxiety disorders, for example).

These drugs are effective against all forms of anxiety, can be used to control epilepsy and for sedation, and are helpful in alcohol detoxification. They work more quickly than antidepressants but have significant drawbacks that make them less attractive. Most can produce dependence (certain of them are popular as drugs of abuse), and for this reason they must be used prudently, particularly if prescribed for longer than several weeks. Xanax is an approved drug for panic disorder but is usually reserved for people who cannot, for some reason, use an SSRI.

BuSpar (buspirone) is a special case: it cannot create dependence and has virtually no abuse potential. It takes longer to start working than other anxiolytics, however, and is generally considered less effective.

Anxiolytics are often used together with other drugs. They may be added early in SSRI treatment, for example, to ease anxiety or difficulty sleeping until the side effects of the antidepressant wane and its benefits gather steam.

*Mood-stabilizing drugs* are primarily given for bipolar disorder (manic depression). Lithium, the oldest of these medications, is still the mainstay of treatment. It is effective in keeping mood stable, but not for treating acute flare-ups. It may also be added in depression treatment, when antidepressants alone aren't effective. Whenever lithium is used, blood levels must be monitored carefully: too low and it doesn't work; too high and toxic reactions (including kidney and liver damage) may result.

Depakote (divalproex sodium) and Tegretol (carbamazepine) were originally developed as anticonvulsants (drugs to control seizures), but they are effective mood stabilizers as well. Both drugs have been used for years in combination with lithium, but Depakote was recently approved as a stand-alone medication for bipolar disorder. It sometimes works when lithium does not and, unlike the older drug, can control the symptoms of acute mania.

A new generation of anticonvulsants, notably Lamictal (lamotrigine) and Neurontin (gabapentin) have come into wider use in recent years, for bipolar disorder and some other conditions as well. Although they appear effective, they have not yet been FDA-approved for these purposes and should generally be prescribed only after tried-and-true drugs fail, and by a psychiatrist who knows them well.

Mood-stabilizing drugs are also used to control symptoms of diverse conditions including personality disorders and post-traumatic stress disorder.

*Antipsychotics* are powerful drugs that are indicated for serious disorders like schizophrenia and manic attacks. The original ones, which include Thorazine (chlorpromazine), Haldol (haloperidol), and Prolixin (fluphenazine) are effective against hallucinations and delusions but can cause such serious side effects as tremor, rigidity, and painful muscle spasms. Prolonged use can lead to tardive dyskinesia, uncontrolled movements of the face and body, which may be irreversible.

In the last decade, a new generation of antipsychotics has largely replaced the older ones. These "atypical" agents, which include Risperdal (risperidone), Zyprexa (olanzapine), and Seroquel (quetiapine), are equally effective for hallucinations and delusions but also seem to improve "negative symptoms" that often occur in schizophrenia, such as lethargy and a flattening of emotions. Most important, they are unlikely to cause the most distressing side effects of their predecessors.

Antipsychotics are being used increasingly in off-label applications (added to other drugs, for example, for depression that doesn't respond to the usual treatment). But even the newer, safer drugs can have serious adverse effects, including dramatic weight gain, and are not to be taken lightly. It's never inappropriate to ask why they are being prescribed, particularly if the doctor chooses one of the older agents.

Pharmacotherapy is an art as well as a science. There's no way to tell in advance which drug will be most effective for which person: about one third of those with depression, for example, will not respond to the first antidepressant prescribed, but most will do well on the second or third. *Polypharmacy* has become increasingly common practice—several drugs are prescribed together to achieve results that a single agent cannot, or to address side effects while maintaining therapeutic benefits.

The more complex the situation becomes, the more important it is to have an expert in charge. While many primary care physicians are competent prescribing SSRIs, few have the experience necessary to go through a series of antidepressant trials to find what works. If you're receiving several drugs at once, a referral to a psychiatrist with particular medication expertise (a "psychopharmacologist") may be in order.

There is abundant information available on-line about virtually all drugs—just enter the name of one in a search engine and scroll through the results. Two sites that have reliable, useful material in a convenient form, including links to more detailed data, are www.mentalhealth.com and www.behavenet.com. The second of these also offers clear explanations of possibly unfamiliar terms.

# Chapter 11

—

# WHAT ELSE?

*Other Therapies*

There's a lot to be said for diversity, among people, biological species, and systems of thought. The panoply of therapies available reflects the vitality of a field that is still exploring the intricacies of human nature, reinventing and redefining itself. New variants, like new biological species, arise, flourish, or pass into obscurity—often leaving their mark in techniques or concepts that are absorbed by the survivors.

Orgone therapy, poetry therapy, primal therapy, feminist therapy, and fixed-role therapy. Morita, Naikan, and allo-centered therapy. Jungian analysis and philosophical counseling. That's just a sample. No brief guide can hope to do justice to this abundance; the few therapies described in this chapter are simply meant to give a sense of some alternatives worth considering now and that bear watching for the future.

## Interpersonal Psychotherapy

When relationships are troubled or lacking, mental health suffers; by the same token, emotional difficulties often lead to interpersonal conflicts and make it hard to maintain friendly or inti-mate connections. It's a self-perpetuating cycle.

Interpersonal psychotherapy (IPT) addresses this dimension of life directly and intensively, in a series of twelve to sixteen weekly sessions. It was first developed (by Gerald Klerman, M.D., and Myrna Weissman, Ph.D., in the mid-1970s) specifically for the treatment of depression, but has since been applied to other prob-lems as well.

The IPT premise is that while interpersonal problems aren't the sole cause of depression, they are an effective focus for treatment. When you work on relationships, the theory goes, mood will improve—and through a cascade of change, symptoms that have ap-parently nothing to do with relationships will get better too. Since all is connected, addressing the part will generalize to the whole.

IPT is a highly systematic therapy. Like cognitive-behavioral therapy, it begins with a detailed personal history, emphasizing the here and now. But the focus is narrower, pinpointing the key rela-tionships in your life. Problems are defined in terms of one or more specific areas:

*Interpersonal disputes* develop at work, at home, and in social relationships. Diverging expectations (a common problem in mar-riage) and faulty communication lead to misunderstanding and con-flict, and poor problem-solving skills make things worse.

*Role transitions* are situations in which you must adapt to new circumstances: the breakup of a relationship, financial reverses, changes at work, even normal events within the life cycle.

*Bereavement* is a normal process—mourning for the death of a loved one—gone wrong. When grieving has been interrupted or is excessive and disabling, it becomes impossible to establish new re-lationships or to be supported by others.

*Interpersonal deficits* characterize a life in which relationships are lacking: they are either distant and shallow or absent altogether.

Once a problem area is identified, the therapist applies tech-niques that often resemble those used in other therapies. In a behav-ioral way, she may help you improve your ability to communicate, develop problem-solving skills to resolve disputes, or examine distorted thought patterns. Like a psychodynamic therapist, she may encourage you to experience painful emotions in the "safe space" of the therapy room.

The focus is generally on present relationships, but especially when these are lacking, the discussion may reach back into the past. Where bereavement is an issue, therapy often attempts to reconstruct the relationship with the deceased, encourage the expression of buried feelings, facilitate the mourning process, and promote new social connections.

Your relationship with the therapist is often an important theme. She won't connect what goes on in the room with your early life or interpret this "transference" as a reflection of your unconscious conflicts but may draw parallels to your problems in the outside world. The therapy can be a testing ground where you try out unfamiliar roles and develop the capacity for more productive relationships.

What makes IPT interesting is how well it appears to work. In a landmark 1989 study of depression sponsored by the National Institute of Mental Health, it was as effective as medication. Over the long term, monthly "booster" sessions worked as well as high doses of an antidepressant in preventing relapse. In the years since, smaller studies have suggested that IPT can be helpful for depression in older people, and in women who are pregnant or have just given birth. A modified version of IPT apparently assists medication in keeping people with bipolar disorder healthy.

Extensions of IPT into the treatment of other disorders in which interpersonal dysfunction plays a role, such as bulimia, social phobia, and post-traumatic stress disorder, have been promising too.

A number of studies have found that improvements continue for the months after therapy is discontinued. This suggests that IPT may work by altering relationships in a way that takes time to pay full dividends.

More detailed information about IPT and its applications is available from the International Society for Interpersonal Psychotherapy [www.interpersonalpsychotherapy.org].

Many therapists trained in IPT are involved in research as well as clinical practice. If you are interested in this kind of therapy, a university department of psychiatry might be a promising place to look.

## EMDR

One of the most intriguing and controversial therapies to emerge in recent years is eye movement desensitization and retraining (EMDR). It was developed in 1987 by Francine Shapiro, Ph.D., and has since become important in the treatment of symptoms related to trauma, particularly post-traumatic stress disorder (PTSD).

EMDR shares with many other approaches the belief that today's dysfunctions often have their roots in events of the past. But it sees the connection in highly specific terms. According to the theory, the brain normally processes unpleasant experiences in an adaptive way—you endure negative emotions and they dissipate. But when trauma overwhelms the brain's ability to cope, memories and emotions remain locked in the nervous system, producing symptoms like depression, anxiety, or the complex emotional disturbances and "flashbacks" of PTSD.

The aim of EMDR is to catalyze the release of locked-up memories. The trapped material is "unfrozen" and reprocessed into a neutral form that no longer causes trouble. When you experience what has been repressed and become desensitized to it, symptoms remit.

The distinctive feature of EMDR is its technique. While you are recalling the trauma or visualizing a problem situation in present-day life, you track a rapidly moving light from side to side (the eye movements of the name) or focus your attention on some other rhythmic stimuli, like hand tapping. According to the theory, this activates memory processes, starting a chain of associations that enables you to reexperience the past vividly and fully, "reprocessing" the trauma in a way that deprives it of toxic power.

Those who practice EMDR stress that this technique is by no means all there is to it. Elements of more conventional therapies also come into play—an essential aspect of treatment is a precise history that focuses on key problems in current life and the triggering situations that bring them on (as in cognitive-behavioral therapy), and some psychodynamic approaches may be used to deal with the reawakened memories. You may need to learn relaxation or other self-soothing techniques before you take on potentially upsetting material.

EMDR should only be administered by an experienced psychotherapist who has received special training in the technique. An estimated thirty thousand therapists worldwide have had such training.

According to its proponents, EMDR often achieves striking improvements in a very short time: two or three sessions in many cases. The most impressive evidence for its effectiveness is in PTSD; the approach is included in the American Psychological Association's list of "probably efficacious" treatments for the disorder, and it is described as effective in the treatment guidelines of the International Society for Traumatic Stress Studies.

There is less evidence for its value in treating phobias, obsessive-compulsive disorder, panic, and depression.

For more information, including instructions for finding a trained therapist, visit the website of the EMDR Institute [www.emdr.com].

## Solution-Focused Therapy

What's wrong is usually more interesting than what's right. Most hit movies aren't *Rebecca of Sunnybrook Farm,* and most people don't seek professional help because they're altogether pleased with life. Traditionally, psychotherapy has devoted a great deal of attention to defining and understanding problems as a necessary prelude to fixing them.

Solution-focused therapy approaches things differently. It cuts right to the chase, spending little time and energy on the subtleties of what's wrong and working from the interesting premise that you already have it in your power to make it right. "You don't need to understand a lock if you have the key" is its philosophy. Therapy is generally done in a limited number of sessions (three to five is typical).

In contrast to many other approaches, this kind of therapy resists thinking of mental difficulties as "disease" or "disorder." Depressed feelings, substance use, uncontrolled anger, and so forth are "complaints," not "symptoms." Viewed in this way, problems look more solvable. Insight isn't necessary before you take action; in fact, to dwell on *why*—on the factors in your past, your genes, or your belief system that make you depressed or anxious or in conflict with your spouse—can be counterproductive. Such explanations, a solution-focused therapist might say, provide more reasons to continue failing than clues to getting what you want.

The therapist takes a restrained role here, asking questions and promoting exploration to help you realize what you already know but may have forgotten, letting you define your own strategy and discover your own solutions.

A key question in this kind of therapy is "What are you doing *right*?" No problem is equally burdensome every moment; even a man who is angry 90 percent of the time may be cheerful and friendly the other 10 percent. Why? Becoming aware of the *exceptions* to the rule can reveal actions, thoughts, *solutions* that are waiting to be maximized. If it works, the idea is, keep on doing it.

When a mood or problem seems constant, you might be asked to go back to a time when it wasn't so intense. What was different then? Or you might be asked to imagine a future in which things are miraculously different; if your problem were to disappear overnight, how could you tell? What would be different?

The therapist may take a behavioral approach, suggesting small changes that will make things slightly better—taking a walk when you're depressed, rather than eating cookies. Little successes increase confidence and motivation and make way for bigger ones. Taking care of one problem in your life can give you the tools for solving others.

Although few trials of solution-focused therapy have been controlled or used rigorous experimental methods, a number of studies suggest that it is quite effective: success rates (for example, clients report reaching their goals) are often in the 60 to 80 percent range. It has been applied to depression, sleep problems, eating disorders, low self-esteem, and alcohol abuse, among other things, in individual and family settings.

More information (targeted to professionals rather than consumers) is available at the Solution-Focused Therapy web page [www.enabling.org].

## Computer Therapy

The possibility of a machine doing therapy has intrigued people ever since computers began their incursions into distinctively human terrain. ELIZA, developed at the Massachusetts Institute of Technology in 1960, was a program that responded to human "patients" with techniques used by real therapists, such as reflection ("You say that you're feeling angry") and clarification ("Why do you think you got so angry?").

ELIZA conducted what could charitably be described as a parody of therapy, following its protocol mindlessly and perhaps showing nothing so much as the value of empathy, creativity, and the human touch.

Both therapy and computers have changed in the last half-century, and what might be called a modern-day descendant of ELIZA shows real promise in the treatment of depression and anxiety disorders. With interactive voice technology, you access a computer by telephone and go through an eight-session course of cognitive-behavioral therapy, answering questions and receiving "homework" assignments tailored to you. The program includes a series of self-help workbooks as well.

One version, COPE, has brought about significant improvements in mild to moderate depression, comparable to what has been seen in trials of live therapy. BT-STEPS, for obsessive-compulsive disorder, showed itself to be as good as face-to-face therapy and better than placebo, in a controlled trial. Patients apparently find both systems as acceptable as live therapists. COPE is commercially available; BT-STEPS is not, although it may be in the near future. Information on both can be found at Health Systems Solutions [www.healthtechsys.com].

Perhaps the most prominent contemporary variation on the cyber-theme, *on-line counseling* or *Internet psychotherapy,* represents the fusion of the human and the technological. According to one recent estimate, about four hundred therapists work over the Internet, holding real-time sessions with patients they've never met.

Among the advantages of on-line counseling are convenience—sessions are more easily squeezed into tight schedules when no travel is involved—and access for people who live in rural or small-town locations. If shame and stigma are issues, you may prefer to participate in therapy when there's no risk of running into neighbors in the therapist's waiting room, or encountering the therapist himself at the supermarket. The cost may be somewhat less, and session length is flexible.

No one would claim, however, that exchanging words electronically is the same thing as being there. Communication, most agree, is impoverished when tone of voice, body language, and other nonverbal nuances are lost. One commercial website overcomes some of these limitations with videoconferencing technology.

Just what happens to the therapeutic relationship in these novel formats is uncertain. Human warmth and intimacy are hard to achieve before the cameras, let alone at the keyboard. But some observers suggest that people are more candid and forthcoming in faceless anonymity, and the computer screen may have a comforting familiarity for many.

There has been no research into the strengths and weaknesses of on-line counseling, but one commercial website suggests that "self-esteem, relationships, workplace problems, parenting, depression, stress and anxiety" are among the most amenable issues. It seems intuitively clear that therapy with someone you never see and who may be hundreds, even thousands of miles away is *not* ideal if you are suicidal, homicidal, self-destructive, or psychotic, or depressed or anxious enough to be in possible need of medication.

The legal issues surrounding on-line counseling are hazy, particularly if the therapist is licensed in another state. Guidelines established by the American Counseling Association [www.counseling.org] and the International Society for Mental Health Online [www.ismho.org] define ethical practice in much the same terms as in face-to-face therapy and specify the particular demands of this format in regard to privacy and informed consent.

If you try on-line therapy, apply the same standards about credentials that you would if you were meeting in the conventional way. Clarify procedural details regarding payment, missed appointments, and the like. To ensure privacy, make sure that sites are secured by encryption technology.

HelpHorizons.com [www.helphorizons.com] is a commercial service that pairs potential patients with licensed therapists who work on-line, by location and schedule; you can arrange video therapy through videoShrink.com [www.videoshrink.com]. Both companies say they authenticate the credentials of participating therapists. A number of interesting articles on on-line therapy are available at the International Society for Mental Health Online.

# Chapter 12

—

# STAYING ON TRACK

*The Course of Psychotherapy*

For all its unique characteristics, psychotherapy has much in common with more mundane projects like taking piano lessons or enrolling in a weight-loss program. You initiate it for a purpose, with the expectation that progress will be made and the understanding that it will eventually come to an end. You're willing to do what you can to make it work, and you look for signs of progress along the way.

There's more involved than just showing up and following directions; the attitude you bring to the enterprise, and how hard you work at it, can make a material difference in how much benefit you derive.

A number of studies, for example, have found that if you have good motivation, high expectations, and an optimistic outlook when entering therapy, you are more likely to profit from the experience. And once therapy has started, active participation pays off. People who talk more or are generally more "involved" in sessions find therapy more satisfactory and enjoy greater relief from specific symptoms and more general improvement.

How to be active and involved? In general, the same advice applies that is often given for rewarding relationships in general: be yourself. If you're shy or active, bold or cautious, bring that into the room with you. "By being yourself with the therapist, you'll let the patterns emerge that are repeated in your life, over and over, and you can examine them together," says psychoanalyst Leon Hoffman, M.D.

Therapy is a partnership, says psychologist Ted Grossbart, and in his experience working partners profit most. "It's like any other task: people who go at it with gusto and perseverance do better than dilettantes." This may mean thinking between sessions about the issues that came up, jotting down notes, and bringing them in, as well as staying alert for material that will be useful to explore, such as dreams and revealing encounters in the real world. Honesty is another key quality. "People who are more ready to be direct and forthright, to go into areas that they find themselves edging away from, are likely to get the most out of it."

In targeted therapies (e.g., cognitive-behavioral), active participation is well defined. "We try to get patients to take notes during or at the end of the session, about things they wish to remember," says cognitive therapist Judith Beck. "Homework" (for example, making a number of contacts with friends or keeping track of thoughts when under stress) is a key component of CBT, and studies have shown that for patients who carry out these assignments, the treatment is substantially more effective.

Going into each session prepared—giving serious thought beforehand to what happened in the course of the week, how your mood and state of mind compare with other weeks, what seems most important to talk about now and what might be worth preparing for in the week to come—enables you to use the time most effectively, Dr. Beck says.

## Is Progress Being Made?

Compared with many other ongoing projects, the course of therapy can seem amorphous once it's under way. It's easier to suggest guideposts for the beginning, where you choose a therapist and look for signs that a productive working relationship is developing (see Chapter 2), and to think in an organized way about the end, or termination phase (see Chapter 14), than to identify landmarks in what often seems a trackless middle section.

Some of this uncertainty simply comes with the territory; except for therapies that are limited to a specific number of sessions (usually at the behest of an outside force, like a health insurance company), it's rarely possible to say just how long it will take to get where you want to go. With certain kinds of therapy, it's customary to project at the outset a rough idea of how much time you'll need to achieve the results you want, but others are more intentionally open-ended. For that matter, your aims may have been more or less broadly defined ("I just want to feel better" versus "I want to be able to take business trips by plane without freaking out") or may change as you get into the process of therapy.

In CBT and similar therapies, identifying the problems you intend to work on and the goals you hope to achieve concretely and specifically ("I want to be more effective at work"; "I want to be more social with people") is a fundamental part of the process. This makes evaluating your progress fairly straightforward; assessing the strides you have made in these directions is usually built into the session itself. The course of therapy may include periodic use of objective tests, such as questionnaires that measure depression and anxiety symptoms, making it possible to answer "How am I doing?" in quantitative terms.

But the issues aren't always so clear-cut, particularly with "exploratory" kinds of therapy—psychodynamic or humanistic—that deal more with emotions, growth, or unconscious conflicts. Psychotherapy is all about becoming more aware and autonomous and developing your capacity to know yourself and trust your judgment. But because feelings are the very material with which you are working, they cannot always be taken at face value to evaluate your progress.

In particular, because resistance to change is a predictable part of such therapy, negative feelings about the process or the therapist are likely to come up from time to time—especially when you're working on material that is painful or difficult to confront. Anger, reluctance to attend sessions, even a conviction of the therapist's incompetence may be signs that *something is happening*—that is, things are going right—but extremely difficult to distinguish from an accurate gut sense that something is wrong.

Sometimes, an inability to appreciate the progress you have made is itself an expression of the problems that brought you into therapy; because of low self-esteem, for example, you can't accept the fact that you're getting better. When you look back over therapy and feel nothing but disappointment, ask yourself whether there's something familiar about the experience. Have you generally tended to undervalue your own abilities, your success, your impact on the world? Often, the observations of close friends or family can correct distortions. Have *they* seen a change for the better?

The short view of therapy is often a useful indication of whether it's on track. How do you feel when you leave the session? It's natural to be troubled or upset sometimes, particularly after dealing with sensitive matters or talking about memories you've been trying to avoid. But in general, you should feel in a better mood, supported, more hopeful and energized when you come out than when you went in.

How would you describe the sessions themselves? Not every one will be a "breakthrough," of course, but at least regularly you might expect to have a sense of discovery, the invigoration of new connections and insights. Does the experience of therapy retain an aura of freshness, of excitement? No matter how long it goes on, the work should be a lively kind of interaction, a real relationship in which you feel connected to and understood by the therapist.

When you have doubts about the progress of therapy, the one best thing you can do is talk about them. "You have to try to be really open with the therapist, to address your dissatisfactions as well as your positive feelings," says Dr. Hoffman. A good therapist will welcome this kind of frankness, take your concerns seriously, and address them thoughtfully. If he gets upset, dismisses what you have to say, explains your doubts away in what seems to you a facile manner, or becomes defensive, then you *do* have a problem. Similarly, if you feel absolutely unable to bring things up, therapy hasn't been working the way it should.

If you've talked it over and still have misgivings, the next step might be to seek an outside opinion—that is, to have a consultation with another mental health professional. It's best to do this openly and in collaboration with the therapist—undeterred by fears that you'll hurt his feelings or alienate his affection. A therapist is, after all, a professional whose principle concern should be your well-being, and like a physician he ought not let personal pride or defensiveness prove an obstacle to your seeking a second opinion. (In fact, you might reasonably expect him to see this as a positive sign that you take the therapy seriously enough to devote energy to making it work.)

Your therapist himself might suggest a consultant, or you can find one by following some of the same steps you used to locate a therapist in the first place: call a professional association or seek a referral from a friend. In general, it's best to talk with someone whose orientation is similar to your therapist's—if she's coming from an incompatible philosophy and uses entirely different techniques, she can't reasonably judge what's happening in your therapy.

Be prepared to describe in detail what brought you into therapy, what you have done thus far, and what problems have led you to consult with her. (Incidentally, it would be unethical for someone you see under these circumstances to offer her own services as a therapist.) If all concerned are willing, the consultant can speak directly to your therapist, to get more light on the situation. It would be highly unusual, however, for the three of you to meet together.

## Is Therapy Going Wrong?

Generally, psychotherapy doesn't have side effects like medication, but if done badly enough, it can be toxic. The very intimacy and intensity of the therapeutic relationship gives it the power to hurt as well as heal. When things go wrong, they can have a sub-tly negative effect on your well-being; at worst they can be down-right traumatic.

Therapists being human, and therapy being an earthbound enter-prise, mistakes do happen and they generally cause no lasting harm. The critical issue is how they're handled: the way your therapist deals with his own mistakes can be the difference between a setback and an opportunity, between confirming his competence or bringing it into question, between strengthening or weakening your bond.

*Item:* Your therapist mispronounces the name of your ex-wife, al-though you've been talking about her in virtually every session for three months. You point this out, a bit testily. Does she apologize, or ridicule your sensitivity on the issue? Or (maybe best of all) apolo-gize and then tactfully suggest exploring your response to her error: do you often feel that she isn't paying sufficient attention to what you say? Is this a feeling you have about other people?

*Item:* You arrive on time for a session but have to wait fifteen minutes while your therapist finishes up with another patient. Again, an apology is in order, perhaps with an explanation about why she's running behind schedule and a promise she'll try to do better (along with a proportional extension of your own session). Here, too, your own irritation or anger at the delay may offer a profitable occasion to explore feelings about having your needs neglected or taking a backseat to those of others. Neither your upset nor the possible rea-sons behind them should be dismissed or taken lightly.

*Item:* The therapist takes a phone call in the midst of your ses-sion. If you consider the intrusion unacceptable and damaging to your sense of safety and ease, he should honor these feelings— that's what voice mail is for. If his "policy" isn't flexible in this re-gard, you may have to look elsewhere. (You probably should be flexible too; for example, if the call is an atypical event, and your therapist explains that one of his patients is having a crisis and he felt he needed to answer that one call.)

Even if his rationale ("My patients need to feel they can get in touch with me; I extend the same consideration to you") is acceptable and you're willing to put up with the interruption, it should be kept to a minimum.

There's a difference between isolated errors and those repeated often enough to create a pattern. If your therapist consistently forgets key details about your life, regularly keeps you waiting, or frequently glances at his watch while you're talking, and you've communicated your feelings about these problems, you must decide whether you can continue to work together.

## Red Flags

Another category of mistakes goes beyond the merely technical. These can put you at risk of significant, even lasting damage and must be taken very seriously. They leave little room for negotiation.

These mistakes involve infractions of the ethical rules that therapy professions establish to maintain standards and to protect clients (see Chapter 3). The most basic among them is the therapist's *fiduciary responsibility*—her obligation to respect your needs and avoid behavior that could be harmful to you.

Like anyone else, a therapist has a right to her feelings. She can find you boring or arrogant, may consider your behavior unspeakable. But she shouldn't say so. Even in the kinds of therapy where "authenticity" on both sides is considered fundamental to the relationship, it must be tempered by sensitivity to your needs and feelings.

A therapist who is highly critical or verbally abusive can erode your self-esteem, undermine your confidence, compound and deepen the traumas that brought you into therapy. She may disapprove of certain of your actions, and can—perhaps should—tell you so. But if she can't sincerely like you as a person, you shouldn't be working together.

Humor may have a place in therapy, but ridicule or sarcasm is never justified. If you don't appreciate "light" remarks, your therapist should speedily adjust her approach.

No matter what kind of therapy you are engaged in, your autonomy should be respected and supported: fostering self-determination is what it ultimately is all about. The therapist's role puts her in a position of influence, and she must use that position with restraint and only in your interests, not to advance her own agenda. This means never imposing her values on you, or exerting pressure to adapt goals that she believes are valid but you don't.

The issue of improper influence has been prominent in recent years in regard to "recovered memories" of childhood abuse. Memory remains a mysterious area, and no foolproof test has been found to distinguish the recollection of something that truly happened from creations of the imagination. It is known, moreover, that memories can be implanted by suggestion, as well as recovered. A therapist who is skilled and well trained and keeps an open mind can be extremely helpful in bringing repressed memories to light. But one who is convinced that depression, anxiety, low self-esteem, eating disorders, and nearly every other ill that the mind or spirit is heir to reflects abuse of which the victim is unaware can cause great harm.

If your therapist tries to convince you of "facts" of which you have no recollection at all, be wary. In particular, the use of hypnosis in the service of recovered memories can be dangerous and unwise.

The most potentially damaging mistakes are violations of the *boundary* that separates therapy from real life. They undermine the atmosphere of safety that makes positive change possible; at worst they can cause lasting harm.

As discussed in Chapter 3, the boundary concept is fluid—up to a point. It generally precludes contact outside the office, but a behavior therapist might well accompany you to a restaurant or take the subway with you, if such situations are the focus of anxiety. For a therapist to attend a patient's family functions is generally a poor idea, but human feeling could argue exceptions—for the funeral of a close relative, for example.

A "boundary crossing" becomes a violation if it forms a pattern, or if it establishes a tone of intimacy. Letting a session run overtime is the kind of lapse few patients would object to (particularly during a crisis), but if habitual, it implies a kind of special treatment that breaks the frame of therapy.

Excessive self-disclosure is a violation of the therapist's role. Making an occasional reference to her own experience to illustrate a point is one thing, but regularly going into detail about her finances, social life, or personal problems is another. At a certain point, just whose needs are being met becomes a question. It may feel gratifying to have your therapist take you into her confidence this way, but it's not in your interest.

Conducting therapy over lunch or in a car may seem innocuous, if irregular, but can be a way station to more extreme things. Boundary violations have a tendency to escalate—leading, in a worst-case scenario, to sexual intimacy.

It has been estimated that between 7 and 12 percent of therapists have had sexual contact with patients. Male therapist/female patient is the most common combination, but the reverse can also occur, as well as same-sex intimacies. *There are no circumstances under which they are justified.* The effects of a therapist's sexual misconduct can be devastating to the patient—it represents a betrayal in many ways similar to incest and can cause comparable harm.

Given the strong emotions that can be aroused in the course of therapy, and the position of trust that the therapist occupies, a patient's consent doesn't mitigate the reality that sexual contact in this situation represents abuse—a fact that is recognized by law in most of the states that have criminalized the behavior.

Sexual misconduct rarely happens entirely out of nowhere, but is usually the culmination of a pattern of boundary violations. Among the warning signs:

• Sexual stories, seductive looks, or allusions to the therapist's own sex life
• Offering alcohol during sessions
• Questionable scheduling practices—repeatedly scheduling you for the last session of the day, or having sessions away from the office

- Inviting you out for lunch, dinner, or other social activities
- Giving (or accepting) significant gifts

Such behavior may seem harmless or even gratifying, but it takes you down a dangerous path. Consult with another therapist without delay.

## Chapter 13

—

# MIND AND MONEY

*Paying for Therapy*

Whoever said "Talk is cheap" probably wasn't in therapy. Actually, it's time that must be paid for; therapists are trained professionals whose work is inescapably time-intensive. To all but the very wealthy or the very poor, money is an irreducible term in the psychotherapy equation.

For many of us, the answer to the question "Who pays?" is, at least in the most immediate sense, a third party. Most health insurance contains some provision for mental health care (often referred to as "behavioral care"), and if you pay substantial premiums or regard health coverage as an important part of your employment package, it seems reasonable to expect psychotherapy to be one of the benefits.

Fair enough. But it's no secret that the American health care system is far from perfect, and that managed care, today's nearly ubiquitous version of health insurance, has come under increasing attack for its deficiencies. Given the nuances of psychotherapy and the personal factors involved, these shortcomings are likely to have more complicated consequences here than, say, when you visit an internist for a sore throat.

How you pay for psychotherapy can determine what therapist you see, what kind of therapy you get, how long it lasts, and how effective it is. Managed care isn't the only way to finance the process; before calling your insurer, get to know some of the issues.

## How Managed Care Works

Back when most people paid their own doctor bills, they paid for therapy as well. This changed with the advent of the *indemnity* form of health insurance, by which you (or your employer, or a combination of both) pay regular premiums and are reimbursed for a portion of your medical expenses. Depending on the nature of the insurance and the size of the premium, this may or may not include psychotherapy.

In the last two decades, concerns about health care costs have given increasing prominence to an arrangement in which the insurer takes a more active role in metering the benefits it pays for. *Managed care* systems bring an explicitly businesslike mentality to the process, defining the specific quantity and quality of health care to which you're entitled. Doctors and other health professionals become "providers," patients are "subscribers," and their dealings with one another are regulated by contract.

Depending on the nature of your contract, you may be limited to "providers" who work for or have special arrangements with your insurer. Whether you receive care, the kind of care you get, and how much of it you get may be determined by neither you nor the health professional but by employees of the insurance company. This can apply to medical tests, referrals to specialists, medication, hospitalization, and surgery. It very often applies to psychotherapy.

In theory, managed care has much in its favor. It keeps those who provide health care *accountable* to a hard-headed system that takes effectiveness seriously. It encourages treatments that work and discourages those that don't. It simplifies such matters as finding specialists. It saves everyone money.

But in the real world, there seems to be a broad consensus (as reflected by calls for health care reform from diverse consumer groups and at every government level) that the system has fallen far short of its ideals. Medical costs have continued to rise, while benefits have tended to dwindle. Choices are limited. The approval or denial of benefits, many maintain, is too often driven by the company's financial interests at the expense of its subscribers.

## Managed Psychotherapy

Generally, health care plans are not eager to pay for therapy. A study sponsored by the National Alliance for the Mentally Ill found that benefits for mental health care declined nearly seven times as steeply, in a single recent decade, as benefits on the whole. In 1986, mental health accounted for 6.2 percent of the total health care benefit; in 1997 it was 3.1 percent.

In virtually all plans, mental health benefits are more closely managed than medical care. A typical contract limits therapy to a specified number (often twenty or thirty) of sessions yearly. But to use these visits, in most plans, you must obtain the approval of a "case manager" employed by the insurance company, who will decide what kind of treatment, if any, you can get. Often, no more than five or ten sessions are approved at once, which means your therapist must report back to the case manager if therapy is to continue beyond that point.

This arrangement influences the whole process of psychotherapy, from the time you start looking for a therapist to the moment that you leave her office for the last time. Many mental health professionals feel that it deeply changes the therapeutic relationship and the nature of therapy itself. Among the most commonly cited matters of concern:

**Choice of therapist.** With the most restrictive kind of managed care, a *health maintenance organization* (HMO), you can only see a therapist (or for that matter, a physician or other health care professional) who participates in the plan, which may well rule out those recommended by friends or others. Few therapists participate in all the plans in their area, and some highly trained professionals avoid them altogether. Other plans are less restrictive but may specify the kind of therapist you can see (for example, a social worker, not a psychiatrist) for a given problem.

In many plans, it is expected that most depression and anxiety disorders will be treated not by health care specialists but by primary care physicians.

**Choice and length of therapy.** Critics contend that managed care organizations press for the use of therapies they consider "cost-effective," without regard to the patient's specific needs. They promote problem-focused treatment and crisis resolution, and tend to disregard the issues that bring many people into therapy—the vulnerabilities and deeper problems that persist after immediate difficulties are resolved. They generally advocate behavioral therapies over psychodynamic or humanistic approaches. According to many observers, they have a bias in favor of medication.

Length is a critical issue. Brief therapy has its uses, and a number of studies have shown that twelve to twenty sessions of certain therapies can be extremely helpful for some people with mood and anxiety disorders. But not even therapists who specialize in short-term therapy suggest that one length fits all. Cutting off all patients after a set number of sessions, in managed care, is often a matter of financial policy, not clinical judgment.

**Quality of therapy.** As studies have documented repeatedly, the relationship with the therapist is a crucial factor in the success of therapy. And it has been widely suggested that when managed care enters the picture, it enters this relationship as well.

Some critics observe that the therapist has a more enduring relationship with the managed care company than with any single patient. Ethics may require your therapist to put your interests first, but this becomes difficult when your needs are pitted against her economic survival. Because managed care companies can drop troublesome "providers" from their rolls, a prudent therapist has a disincentive to appeal or question its judgments.

In a number of surveys, therapists have reported that they take less satisfaction in their work when it is under the control of a third party. Some admit that they look forward to cancellations under these circumstances and feel less "concern" for clients who they know may leave therapy at the whim of a case manager. In one study of one thousand Massachusetts therapists, two thirds said they have terminated therapy, whether or not the patient was ready, to comply with managed care rules.

Some therapists have said that managed care demands have led them to use therapy approaches that they do not consider optimal, and for which they have less affinity and training. A recent article in the *Clinical Social Work Journal* went as far as to question, "Is managed mental health treatment psychotherapy?"

**Privacy.** An argument can be made that the worst casualty of managed mental health care is privacy. If you're reluctant to bare your personal problems to a therapist, you probably won't feel any better explaining them to an unseen case manager who may or may not have mental health training. Your willingness to speak openly and spontaneously during therapy, a key part of the process, is arguably compromised by the realization that your therapist may have to discuss your case with third parties to get continued benefits. If you get insurance through your employer, the stakes are heightened.

Legislation recently enacted by Congress strengthens protection for the privacy of medical records generally. It requires professionals and insurance companies to explain how they use, keep, and disclose patient information, and forbids the release of information without your consent.

In practice, however, the new law has serious limitations. It doesn't prevent health insurers from making treatment contingent on your agreement to release parts of your record for "routine" uses (for example, decisions about the necessity of continued therapy), which makes "consent" something less than voluntary. It allows health plans to use or disclose patient information for "purposes of health care treatment, payment and operations"—vague conditions that may include marketing.

The legislation requires companies to "adopt privacy procedures," but in today's wired world, no one can say where information will end up. When a "provider" bills an insurer electronically, the bill (possibly with details of treatment) passes through several clearing-houses, which typically store the information for several weeks and are not subject to government regulation.

In a survey by a California county psychological association, cited in *The Wall Street Journal,* more than one third of clinicians said they had clients who had opted not to have therapy or discontinued it prematurely because of anxiety about privacy.

## If You Use Managed Care ⁻

Some plans are clearly better than others, and if you have a choice through your job or are purchasing coverage on your own, keep in mind these recommendations from the American Psychiatric Association:

By paying higher premiums or more out-of-pocket, you may be able to enroll in a *point of service* (POS) plan that enables you to choose health care professionals freely, rather than being tied to the HMO network. (Check the details of the plan's mental health coverage. It may be more restrictive than for medical care.)

Opt for a plan, if you can find one, that requires less stringent or no preapproval for psychotherapy. Again, remember that even plans allowing you to see medical specialists without a referral often make exceptions for mental health care.

Find out from your therapist and your insurer just what protections are in place to guard privacy. If you're asked to sign forms to release information, make sure they're time-limited. Your therapist should be willing to restrict the information she gives to case managers to the minimum necessary for their decisions—make sure this is understood. You have a right to see such reports before they're released.

Do a quality check. The National Commission on Quality Assurance [www.ncqa.org] accredits managed care organizations that meet their standards and offers some information on how they stack up in some measures of performance. Their on-line ratings are sketchy but worth viewing.

The National Coalition of Mental Health Professionals and Consumers [www.nomanagedcare.org] is an advocacy organization devoted to improving coverage for mental health care. Its *Mental Health Consumer Protection Manual* provides useful tips on solving insurance problems. You can purchase it or find substantial excerpts on the coalition's website.

Among their suggestions:

• Be assertive if you feel you've been denied benefits unfairly. Cause a company time-consuming problems, and they're likely to give you what you need.

• Think like a consumer. If you don't get satisfaction from low-level personnel (many of whom are only empowered to say no), insist on talking to a supervisor, a medical director, an executive. Get the names, titles, and credentials of the people you deal with, and make it clear you'll hold them responsible.

• Document all your encounters, including failed attempts to contact the company. Although the applicable laws vary from state to state, it is almost always legal to tape a telephone conversation in the United States if you obtain the consent of all the parties to the call in advance.

## Not All Care Is Managed Care

It's possible to circumvent the managed care issue entirely and get psychotherapy the old-fashioned way—by paying for it out-of-pocket. In fact, this is an option that has considerable and possibly increasing appeal. In surveys by two publications, *Psychotherapy Finances* and *Practice Strategies,* therapist-readers reported that nearly half of their income comes from patients' direct payments.

Privacy concerns motivate many people to pay their own way. In a professional meeting of psychiatrists not long ago, a speaker described the mother of a boy with a severe anxiety disorder who insisted on paying for her child's treatment in cash rather than filing an insurance claim, for fear that a record of his illness might make it hard for him to be insured later. His audience was in general agreement that her worries were not unfounded. The same goes for concerns about the risk of ineffectually guarded records getting into the hands of employers.

The free choice of therapist and of therapy are other reasons to pay for your own treatment. Many people who want to pursue therapy that lasts more than several months will end up funding it themselves.

The out-of-pocket cost of psychotherapy varies widely, depending on geography, training, and setting; between $80 and $150 per session is typical. Psychiatrists generally charge the highest fees, clinical psychologists somewhat less, and social workers less than that.

If money is an issue, consider low-cost alternatives, such as community mental health centers (call your state Department of Mental Health to find them), or university clinics staffed by trainees in psychotherapy programs. Psychoanalytic institutes (see Chapter 5) generally have sliding-scale clinics where you can get long-term psychodynamic therapy or even analysis.

Many psychotherapists in private practice are willing to negotiate fees, even to discount them substantially, for prospective patients who feel they will have difficulty paying the full amount. It's a subject to bring up when interviewing prospective therapists. Creative arrangements, including barter (which raises ethical questions, however) and partially deferred payments, are not uncommon.

For that matter, there's nothing wrong with tapping your health insurance benefits for what they're worth and then continuing on your own. As long as you remember that what an insurance company considers adequate treatment is based more on fiscal than on clinical factors. The most insidious danger of the managed care system is buying into the belief that limited treatment is all that's necessary, or that medication is better than therapy, simply because it suits a corporation's balance sheet.

"I've heard patients say, 'I should have been better in ten sessions. It's my fault I'm not. Nothing can help me,'" says Karen Shore, Ph.D., founder and past president of the National Coalition of Mental Health Professionals and Consumers. "The truth is, when people have more money, they spend longer in therapy."

Do your own cost-benefit analysis. If you feel that a year of therapy is likely to make you happier, improve your relationships, or enhance your capacity for work, is it worth the four to six thousand dollars it will probably cost?

*Chapter 14*

—

# THE LAST CHAPTER

*Bringing Therapy to a Close*

It's often hard to bring any significant undertaking to an end, even one that involves some struggle and stress. When it's over, a part of life will be over. Activity will give way to absence.

Therapy is no exception. No matter how much you've accomplished, the last chapter is liable to be edged with ambivalence. Is it really time to leave? Have I given it all that I can? Have I gotten everything I could? Will there be hard feelings? Psychotherapy is, to repeat a point that was made before, a relationship, usually a close and meaningful one, and it's not often easy to say good-bye—even when both parties agree it's for the best, and the parting means it has served its purpose.

At the same time, the end of therapy (an event traditionally given the rather ominous name *termination*) can be a fruitful occasion. It's not simply the moment when therapy stops, but the final phase of a process. It can be a time to consolidate gains, address important issues, make preparations for the future that will pay dividends in years to come.

## Is It Time to Leave?

The constraints of managed care may have had, upon the whole, a dolorous effect on psychotherapy, but they unquestionably simplify termination. If you're relying on health insurance to pay the bill, when your case manager decides that therapy is finished (no matter how nontherapeutic her motives), it's finished.

No matter who pays, only one fourth to one third of people stay in therapy beyond the eighth session; presumably those who drop out simply feel better or don't see the point of continuing. Under these circumstances, it's unlikely to be a very complex decision.

But after more sustained therapy the issue may be less clear. Termination is usually motivated by one of the same two reasons: you feel that therapy isn't working, or you feel that it's worked. The first of these was considered at some length in the previous chapter, and the conclusions there bear repeating: when you're dissatisfied with what's happening or doubtful about how well the approach or the therapist matches your needs, discuss your misgivings fully if at all possible, make modifications if you can, and change directions accordingly.

Ending therapy that has apparently served its purpose is a happier occasion but not without ambiguities of its own. If you came to a therapist just for help through a well-defined crisis and the crisis has been resolved, there's nothing much to do except say good-bye.

It's not as simple when therapy has been applied to more extensive problems (for example, depression, work difficulties, or anxiety). If the approach was a highly structured one like cognitive-behavioral therapy, explicit goals were probably established at the outset; at the point where they seem to have been accomplished and maintained long enough to appear reasonably solid, the possibility of termination naturally arises.

But goals change and new issues frequently arise in the course of therapy, and these may deserve discussion. "The question becomes whether there's anything else you want to work on," says cognitive therapist Robert Leahy, Ph.D. "After two or three months, a patient may no longer be depressed or anxious but may want to continue working on what makes him or her vulnerable, and a sense of what to do if difficulties recur."

And there's another therapy goal that's harder to pin down: personal growth. Having experienced some specific benefits of therapy, "a lot of people come to feel that it can enhance their lives—make relationships better, help with decisions, improve self-esteem, offer a way to get more out of life," Dr. Leahy says. The process is fundamentally open-ended, and it's not easy to know when you've taken it as far as you can, or want to. But this is a judgment no one else can make.

Growth and self-realization are what humanistic therapies (like gestalt or person-centered therapy) are all about. With these, the therapist is scrupulously nondirective, staying out of the way as you set your own agenda and creating a supportive environment in which you can seek and find what you need. That philosophy continues to the end.

"Trusting the client means letting him decide when and how to leave," says person-centered therapist Jerold Bozarth. "Some people just disappear, some talk about it for a while, some pop up a few years later." Termination grows organically out of the therapy process, like the ripening of a fruit and its eventual separation from the tree.

It's similar in family therapy: when the structure of the family has changed to function better and support its members, it essentially takes over the work of therapy. "In my experience, formal termination rarely happens," says social worker Phoebe Prosky. "People eventually forget to come, or stop scheduling sessions."

In psychodynamic therapy, you may begin to think of termination when you start to wonder if you've said everything to the therapist that you have to say. You feel confident that you can take care of your problems, and ready to accept responsibility for your decisions. You've started to see your therapist more realistically, neither idealized for his wisdom nor the object of anger for his limitations.

In this situation, says psychologist James McMahon, Ph.D., "I'll suggest that the patient take a long walk, spend a few hours mulling over the question of whether it's time to go. Whatever he decides, I'll support."

If your therapist doesn't agree that termination is advisable at this time, he may point out things that you still might want to work on, or suggest further issues to explore on your own. He should not force the issue and, above all, should refrain from making predictions about a relapse or other troubles that lie ahead should you be so unwise as to discontinue his care.

On the other hand, it may be the therapist who broaches the subject of termination. "I'll bring it up if I find that I'm losing interest in the patient," Dr. McMahon says. "If I no longer feel the intense involvement and caring that I did, it's a sign to me that therapy is probably finished."

## The Process of Leaving

Some people decide that they're finished with therapy, announce it at their next session, and that's that. This isn't necessarily bad—it may be a healthy act of assertiveness and independence. But if you're tempted to handle termination this way, you might want to ask yourself why such an abrupt departure is necessary. Is the act of leaving so painful that you're unwilling to prolong the experience? Is there still an attachment to your therapist that makes it hard to separate in a more gradual way?

If you hate extended good-byes, there's rarely much harm in treating the close of therapy simply as a painful parting to put behind you. But it could mean depriving yourself of a useful opportunity to derive a final, substantial benefit from the months or years of work you've invested in the relationship. Often this is a particularly rich part of therapy, "a charged moment . . . a last chance to really look at things," says Dr. McMahon.

What you can look at is *parting* itself—which is a part of life, inseparable from growth and change, literally from our first moments on earth to our last. Even when separation is an act of independence and triumph, it is weighted with loss: parents' tears at weddings are not just expressions of joy. And many of the things that trouble us throughout life are bound up with difficulties in letting go: we can't realize our potential because we find it impossible to leave the comfortable and familiar behind; we've separated (from home, from childhood, from a marriage that didn't make it) but cling to its remnants in a state of semiattachment that interferes with new relationships or greater maturity.

We have many separations but few opportunities to experience them thoughtfully, in a situation designed expressly for that purpose. Interpersonal therapy and brief dynamic therapy, whose focus is on relationship difficulties, consider separation important enough to devote up to a third of their limited sessions to the process. In less structured kinds of therapy, a termination date may be set a month or two in the future, allowing time to explore issues that the prospect of parting awakens: most often loss, dependence, abandonment, and guilt. Or sessions may be tapered: from once weekly to every second, and then every third week—this gives the opportunity to experience and consider the process of leaving and to confirm your ability to make it on your own.

Misgivings about termination are particularly worth investigating. "A lot of clients have a black-and-white view of independence," says psychotherapist James Pretzer, Ph.D. "They're afraid they'll be pushed out of therapy before they're ready. Others have a fear of rejection and act as though termination is a personal response to them. When such strong reactions arise, it's good to make them explicit and to talk them through."

Often a patient who feels abandoned when his therapist talks about parting has responded similarly to earlier situations, and the final phase of therapy provides a matchless opportunity to delve into this theme and gain insights that will lessen its power over future relationships.

Sometimes, the process of termination is complicated by fears of hurting the therapist's feelings. In addition to keeping reality factors in mind—friends part when something is wrong, but therapy isn't a friendship, and a sign of its success is your ability to end it and satisfy your needs with real-life relationships—you might take the opportunity to work through a tendency to put others' feelings before your own. If considered honestly and directly, anxiety about separation might allow you to explore feelings about death.

It's also a time to look closely at your satisfaction and dissatisfaction with the therapy itself. Have you gotten what you wanted out of it, or do you feel disappointed? A lot of pop-psychology books promote unrealistic expectations of radical release from the pain of existence, a cure for all that ails you. But life is imperfect, and "ordinary human unhappiness" (Freud's description of the goal of psychoanalysis) is as good as it gets, even after the best of therapy. Part of wisdom is accepting what can't be changed, and perfectionism needn't keep you in therapy pursuing an impossible dream, or leave you angry that it was never realized.

The end of therapy is a time to look toward the future—realistically, accepting that the problems that brought you there have not been obliterated without a trace; that you're still fundamentally you, and perhaps still susceptible to difficulties like depression or anxiety. But also confidently, knowing that you're better equipped, as a result of your experience, to deal with them if they recur.

"During termination, we work on relapse prevention," says Dr. Pretzer. "I try to help clients anticipate what situations might be difficult for them to handle, and to think through in advance how they would deal with them." Forewarned is forearmed; if you became depressed when you were laid off, you can leave therapy with a game plan for dealing with future career reversals and the feelings of failure that come along with them.

If you've been troubled by conditions that tend to return, like depression or generalized anxiety, a most vital kind of self-knowledge acquired in therapy could be awareness of your own specific early warning signs, and a repertoire of strategies to head them off: making an effort to stay in contact with friends when you feel the tendency to withdraw, for example, or being sure to sleep regular hours when demands at work or at home are heavy.

When you leave therapy, you're on your own but not alone. Most therapists make it clear that their door is always open, and it's not unusual to return for an occasional "booster session" in a particularly stressful time, or even for a few weeks or months to stop a backward slide. More generally, a positive experience in therapy makes you familiar with a resource that will be there if you need it again.

Life is full of difficulties, and we all tend to slip into old habits under stress. A trauma or loss or simply starting a new phase of your life may bring troubles, old or new, to the surface. The last lesson you might take away from therapy is that it's no sign of weakness to recognize when you need help, and knowing where to find it is a solid source of strength.

*Appendix*

—

# WHAT'S WRONG WITH YOU?

*A Brief Guide to Diagnosis*

Giving a name to your problems is often the first step to solving them. It's when vague feelings of sadness, lack of energy, and difficulty sleeping lead you to ask, "Am I depressed?" that you're likely to seek help.

For a therapist, diagnosis is a tool to facilitate organized thinking. It helps her understand your difficulties in the context of her training and her experience, and plan appropriate treatment. The scientific studies whose data guide treatment decisions would not be possible without general agreement about definitions of "panic disorder," "major depression," and "schizophrenia." There's an economic function too: those who pay for health care are more likely to foot the bill for what has been labeled "major depressive episode" than for sadness or malaise.

A label can mislead, however, suggesting more than it actually means. In medicine, a diagnosis typically identifies the pathological process and possibly the cause of the disease: "pneumococcal pneumonia" means a well-defined condition of the lungs, caused by a particular microorganism, that is likely to respond to specific treatments. But in mental health, a diagnosis is descriptive, not explanatory. To say that a person has "panic disorder" is simply giving a title to a collection of subjective experiences and objective events (an overwhelming feeling of fear, accompanied by physical symptoms like racing heartbeat, sweating). Although doctors and scientists have thoughts about the cause of panic, these remain conjecture.

Mental health problems are generally called "disorders" rather than diseases in recognition of this uncertainty factor: "depression" can have a number of different causes, take different forms, and require different treatments, and the diagnosis is properly regarded as a starting point, not a full explanation.

There's also the risk of reducing a person to his diagnosis: someone with schizophrenia all too easily becomes a "schizophrenic"; one with a phobia is "phobic." Remember that a label is always a simplification. If you have an anxiety disorder, that's not *all* you are; it's just a part, if a particularly troublesome part, of your overall identity. Labels can be misused to dehumanize: calling someone a "borderline personality" dismisses the complexity and richness of the human being; it may be a value judgment cloaked in an authoritative term. A good therapist will use all her skills to understand the individual before her, and to treat that person, not a disorder.

For that matter, diagnoses are not written in indelible ink. The American Psychiatric Association's *Diagnostic and Statistical Manual of Mental Disorders,* the classification system used by the mental health field, relies on committees of experts to define disorders. In the four editions that it has gone through since the early 1950s, the number of "disorders" has burgeoned from less than one hundred to nearly four hundred; many have been subdivided into more nuanced subspecies, while others have merged, changed their names, or simply ceased to be recognized.

In part, this is because psychiatric diagnosis has a social as well as a medical function; by labeling something a "disorder" we flag it as abnormal, undesirable, and in need of treatment. Homosexuality was a "disorder" up until the 1970s; today it is not. The behavior didn't change, but society did.

With very few exceptions, psychiatric "disorders" aren't qualitatively different from normal behavior and experience, but represent the far end of a spectrum. We all experience anxiety under appropriate conditions—it probably evolved as a warning system to mobilize us against danger. It becomes a disorder when the response is too easily aroused, and makes life harder, not safer. Most everyone feels energetic, confident, and optimistic sometimes, low and lethargic other times. If one or both of these tendencies are exaggerated and long-lasting, they become a "mood disorder."

Cutting through the complex categories, fine distinctions, and detailed criteria that professionals use, the key question that determines whether or not your feelings, behavior, and thought patterns constitute a disorder that needs treatment is a common-sense one: do they cause you significant distress, or interfere with your ability to function socially, personally, at work?

An idea of what may be wrong can not only help you decide to seek help but suggest what kind of help will be best. The following discussion of the most common mental disorders is based on definitions in the fourth edition of the *Diagnostic and Statistical Manual of Mental Disorders* (*DSM-IV*).

More detailed information about specific psychiatric conditions can be found at the website of the National Institute of Mental Health [www.nimh.nih.gov].

## Depression

This is the most widespread of the major disorders, afflicting one fifth of American women and one tenth of men in the course of their lives. Perhaps because we toss the term around casually, saying we're "depressed" when we're unhappy or discouraged, a lot of people discount the seriousness of real depression. It is estimated that just one third of Americans with the condition seek treatment.

One of the key distinctions between everyday blues and a clinical depression is duration; if a mood has been troubling you every day or most of every day for two weeks or longer, check it out.

True depression means more than a sad feeling. Your emotional state may be numb or empty rather than "down." And along with your bad mood come distressing thoughts and feelings of guilt or worthlessness. A sense of the pain and futility of life can prompt thoughts of suicide. You may lose interest or pleasure in your usual amusements. Your energy level is off-kilter—you may feel agitated and restless, constantly fatigued, or simply slowed down. It may become hard to concentrate or think clearly; decisions that you normally make without much thought become unaccountably difficult.

Your body is troubled as well as your mind; changes in sleep patterns (insomnia or excessive sleeping) and appetite (along with noticeable weight gain or loss) are frequent hallmarks of depression. Headache, joint or muscle aches, and abdominal pain are often part of the picture.

Most people with depression don't have all these symptoms. Psychiatrists use a checklist—more than half of them, together, merits a diagnosis of "major depressive episode." But even a few, if they last for more than two weeks and interfere with your life, should prompt you to consider professional help. If you're finding it extremely difficult to go on with your work or relate to others, or if you have suicidal thoughts, don't delay.

While the grief that follows a serious loss, particularly the death of a loved one, may resemble depression, some hallmarks are usually absent: suicidal thoughts, feelings of worthlessness, a sense of being physically slowed down. There's no timetable for mourning, but if you don't feel any better several months after your loss, it may be wise to speak with a professional.

Depression is particularly insidious and easy to miss if it is chronic, a condition called "dysthymia." Generally, the symptoms are a more subtle version of those seen in major depression—low mood, disturbed sleep or appetite, poor energy level, feelings of hopelessness or worthlessness, difficulty concentrating or making decisions. But they have persisted (at least most of the time) for two years or longer.

People with dysthymia are unlikely to be disabled or in crisis—they can function, but not nearly as well as they might if unburdened by their condition. They are often extremely conscientious workers but are kept in low-level jobs by devastating feelings of inadequacy and other effects of the illness. They may lead withdrawn and lonely lives or remain in unsatisfying marriages.

If you've been plagued by such mood problems for as long as you can remember, you've probably forgotten that life can be any different: a common reaction of people successfully treated for dysthymia is surprise at how much the world has to offer. And treatment *can* be successful, even when depression has lasted for decades, as several large recent studies have shown.

Depression often recurs. If you've had it before, be alert for signs that the condition is returning: prompt treatment can nip it in the bud. Problems sleeping are often an early tip-off.

Among the effective treatments for depression are cognitive-behavioral therapy, interpersonal therapy, and pharmacotherapy.

Detailed information about the various forms of depression can be found at www.psycom.net/depression.central.html, a site created by Ivan Goldberg, M.D., a psychiatrist and clinical psychopharmacologist in New York City.

## Anxiety Disorders

Everyone experiences anxiety, an unpleasant state with both physical and emotional elements. We're wired to mobilize the "fight or flight" response in the face of danger: the heart accelerates, muscles tense, breathing becomes quick and shallow. Along with the physical changes come feelings of dread, foreboding, intense fear. Anxiety becomes a disorder when the response arises even in the absence of danger, like a car alarm that is triggered by the vibrations of every passing truck, or that goes off spontaneously. An estimated 16 percent of people suffer from one or another anxiety disorder in the course of a year.

You can have an anxiety disorder without knowing it. When the symptoms are fairly subtle—not overwhelming as much as quite unpleasant—the response is often to avoid the activities that bring them on. In other words, you may gradually circumscribe your world to remain free from distress: you stay home more, pass up events where there are likely to be crowds, or turn down assignments that require presentations, perhaps without really knowing why.

When its most dramatic manifestations are physical, anxiety can be mistaken for a medical problem. The chest pains that may come with runaway anxiety are responsible for many a trip to the emergency room. Often it is diagnosed only after a long and fruitless series of visits to medical specialists.

Detailed information about anxiety disorders and their treatment is available from the Anxiety Disorders Association of America [www.adaa.org].

Anxiety disorders can look very different from one another, depending on the expression of the anxiety and the situations that bring it on.

*Generalized anxiety disorder* (GAD) is the "worry disease." It's a chronic state of tension (more days than not, for at least six months) that can extend to anything or everything. People with this condition are generally fearful of what the future may bring; they fret constantly about the safety of their children, the state of their tires, their health, their investments. They let the least mishap or ominous sign trigger a bout of nervous preoccupation. Muscle tension, fatigue, irritability, restlessness, and troubled sleep are common symptoms.

A little worry is a wonderful thing; it keeps you alert and prevents careless mistakes. But the worry of GAD serves no useful function. In fact, it can cloud thinking, interfere with concentration, and make life generally difficult.

A particularly intense episode of anxiety, in which fear is accompanied by physical symptoms, is a *panic attack*. Palpitations, sweating, trembling, feelings of choking or smothering, chest pain, dizziness, or nausea are among the most common manifestations.

People in the grip of a panic attack are often terrified they're going crazy, losing control, or dying.

Many things can bring on panic attacks, such as drugs (including caffeine) and medical conditions. When they appear without apparent cause, and the sufferer worries continually about when they'll come back or starts to change her behavior to circumvent them or to make sure she's in a "safe" place if they do happen, it's called *panic disorder*. Panic disorder isn't common, but it isn't rare either; 1 to 2 percent of the population will suffer from it in a given year.

A *phobia* is anxiety attached to a particular object or situation and which commonly leads to avoidance. (The fear must be disproportionate; someone who stays away from dark alleys in bad neighborhoods is displaying prudence, not a disorder.) A *specific phobia* is highly focused, directed against cats (ailurophobia), heights (acrophobia), spiders (arachnophobia), or any of a hundred other things. Even apparently limited phobias can extend in widening circles (avoiding places where a cat *may* be encountered), or involve substantial inconvenience (fear of flying).

*Agoraphobia* is commonly described as anxiety about being in public, but it more specifically relates to places from which it is difficult to escape: crowds, theaters, bridges, public transportation. This in turn reflects the need to be able to withdraw or get help in the event of a panic attack or paniclike symptoms (violent stomach upset, dizziness), and often develops after such episodes. It is frequently seen in connection with panic disorder.

*Social phobia* (also known as *social anxiety*) is quite common, affecting an estimated 3 to 12 percent of people during their lives. It is a marked, persistent fear of being exposed to the scrutiny of others—a fear of humiliation. It's a vicious cycle: anxiety in feared situations causes physical symptoms (like trembling), which then become the focus of fear (people will see and laugh at this). Social phobia can take the form of general, extreme shyness and lead to isolation, as occasions that might arouse anxiety are avoided. It can also appear as performance anxiety: "stage fright" is a form of social anxiety.

Just where normal jitters become social anxiety is sometimes hard to say. Most people will be shy in certain unfamiliar situations; when surveyed about what they fear, many in the general population rank "public speaking" ahead of death. The key is the intensity of the distress, or the tendency to avoid situations because of it.

The most striking feature of *obsessive-compulsive disorder* (OCD) is not anxiety per se, but persistent thoughts and/or actions. Obsessions are recurrent, distressing thoughts, impulses, or images: you feel you're about to do something terrible, or you can't stop imagining dire mishaps befalling those you love. Compulsions are repetitive actions ("rituals") that you feel driven to perform, although you know they don't really make sense: endless hand washing, repeated counting, making sure the door is locked or the stove turned off. Anxiety is what gives the rituals their power: they're performed to keep uncomfortable feelings at bay.

Most of us engage in similar behaviors from time to time: we get up one more time to make sure the windows are closed; we can't push a troubling thought out of our heads. We observe ritualistic superstitions—even as adults we may avoid stepping on sidewalk cracks. But in OCD, the thoughts and rituals take up a good deal of time (more than an hour a day), cause great distress, and get in the way of normal life.

Many people with this disorder are tortured by feelings of shame; their behavior seems "crazy" even to themselves, and they go to great lengths to keep it secret. They're too ashamed to seek treatment, or delay it for as long as possible—on average, seven years after the appearance of symptoms. This is particularly unfortunate, because both psychotherapy and medication are extremely effective for OCD.

Information about OCD is available from the Obsessive-Compulsive Foundation [www.ocfoundation.org].

Events that threaten grave bodily harm are bound to have repercussions, for witnesses as well as victims. It's natural to shy away from similar situations, to be unusually nervous, to have nightmares. But the disturbance usually remits in time. If it lasts longer than a month, you may have *post-traumatic stress disorder* (PTSD).

PTSD is often associated with war, but it can also develop after a disaster like an earthquake or fire, a physical assault, including rape, an automobile accident, or simply the receipt of shocking news, such as the unexpected death of a close friend. Estimates of its prevalence range from 1 to 14 percent, depending in part on the population sampled. Symptoms include reexperiencing the event (in nightmares or flashbacks, for example); avoiding things that remind you of the trauma; and hypersensitivity to arousal—jumpiness, difficulty falling asleep, anger outbursts.

Anxiety disorders generally respond best to specific kinds of cognitive-behavioral therapy and to pharmacotherapy. For social phobia, group therapy is helpful as well.

## *"Addictions"*

The term *addiction* is applied nowadays to any behavior that we're not happy about but find hard to control ("He's addicted to video games"), or even just things we particularly enjoy ("I'm addicted to watching the Yankees"). A fruitlessly lingering romantic attachment is "addiction to a person," and a tendency to waste money at the mall is "shopping addiction."

Semantic inflation aside, it's still a useful concept, particularly in its original application to intoxicating substances, although for clarity many in the field prefer the more precise terms *dependence* and *abuse.*

Abuse represents the habitual consumption of alcohol or drugs in a way that causes significant impairment or distress, and continues despite recurrent legal problems, social or relationship problems, difficulties at school or work, and hazardous behavior linked to it.

Abuse is often a way station to *dependence,* which approximates the popular meaning of addiction: use of alcohol or drugs (this can include nicotine) in a way that is no longer controllable. Physical signs of dependence are the need for increasing amounts of the substance ("tolerance") and extreme physical distress when it isn't available ("withdrawal"). It suggests psychological dependence when alcohol or drugs take over one's life—much time is spent getting it, getting high, and getting over its effects, while other activities are neglected; you often use more alcohol or drugs than you intend, your attempts to cut down are unsuccessful, and you keep on doing it despite unquestionably negative effects on your health.

Recognizing that you have a problem is the first, often hardest part of dealing with substance abuse and dependence. Among treatments that may help are pharmacotherapy and family therapy. But dealing with substance abuse often involves much besides (or instead of) psychotherapy; this is one place where self-help, that is, Twelve-Step Programs like Alcoholics Anonymous, are often quite effective.

Therapy can be a critical element, however, when substance problems occur in the context of other mental disorders. While alcohol and drug abuse and dependence have a life of their own, they often begin in attempts to "self-medicate" anxiety or depression, and treating these conditions can be a key strategy for taming the substance problem and keeping it from coming back.

Whether it's helpful or misleading to call other distressing behaviors "addictions" is a matter of debate. Some experts feel that when excessive, uncontrollable gambling, eating, sexual behavior, or the like follow the pattern of substance dependence (tolerance, withdrawal), they are essentially nondrug versions of the same thing, and note that they often respond to Twelve-Step self-help programs.

It is important to keep in mind, however, that what looks like addiction may be a manifestation or complication of another psychological condition; by its nature, obsessive-compulsive disorder involves actions over which the sufferer feels nearly powerless and which may serve no purpose or even cause harm: hoarding magazines and newspapers, for example, or endlessly washing hands to the point of skin damage. The boundless need for frequent, ill-advised encounters of "sexual addiction" may reflect a personality disorder.

*Gambling addiction* is classified by many psychiatrists as an "impulse-control disorder"; a key characteristic is an inability to rein in the drive to achieve immediate satisfaction or release of tension. *Food addiction* seems uncontrollable and self-destructive, like substance abuse, but may reflect an eating disorder like bulimia.

## Personality Disorders

Each of us is a unique mix of traits and qualities; some people tend to be suspicious, others standoffish, ambitious, self-absorbed, theatrical. Within limits, most personalities are flexible; we can adjust our approach to the situation at hand, and modulate our personality traits to get along with others. But when particular traits dominate, upset the healthy balance, and are so rigid that they cause dysfunction in our lives and distress to ourselves and others, they are said to constitute a *personality disorder.*

This is an ambiguous area in mental health. Theories of personality are at the heart of psychology and reflect fundamental (and divergent) beliefs and assumptions about human nature and the sources of its diversity. To the ancient Greeks, personality was largely determined by bodily fluids, or "humors," which had to be in balance: a preponderance of "black bile" caused a melancholy temperament; "yellow bile" in excess produced an angry person. Today's *DSM-IV* recognizes ten ways in which the personality can be out of whack, but some experts have developed systems that subdivide them into many more.

Generally, a personality disorder reflects an exaggeration of a normal, adaptive trait: a degree of suspiciousness and distrust often comes in handy on occasion, but too much, all the time means *paranoid personality disorder;* it's good to have high standards, but when perfectionism and the need for control predominate it becomes *obsessive-compulsive personality disorder.* Where "normal" ends and "disorder" begins is often a matter of some debate.

More so than other psychological problems, personality disorders are by definition deeply ingrained and pervade every corner of your life—in particular, your relationships with others, your emotional responses, and your control over your impulses. This can make them all the more difficult to see; people with personality disorders often get along in life, if not terribly well, and their problems may cause more grief to others than to themselves.

Among them: *Histrionic personality* is characterized by excessive emotion and the need to be the center of attention. These people are often quite attractive to others but shallow in their relationships.

Those with *borderline personality disorder* are erratic; their feelings are mercurial and often overwhelming, and frequently lead to impulsive, even self-destructive behavior. Their relationships are highly unstable; the person they idolize today may be demonized tomorrow.

*Antisocial personality disorder* involves a deep disregard for the rules of society, the laws, and the rights of others. These people lack empathy—the feelings of their fellow humans simply have no reality for them—and are untroubled by conscience. The "psychopath" generally fits this description: many spend a good deal of time in jail.

People with *avoidant personality disorder* are essentially terrified of other people; their bone-deep fear of criticism and rejection makes them withdrawn and isolated. Those with *schizoid personality disorder,* on the other hand, simply have no use for others; they seem emotionally cold, lack friends, and appear indifferent to praise or criticism.

We use the term *narcissistic* casually, to denigrate selfish or vain behavior. But *narcissistic personality disorder* takes this to extremes. Self-esteem becomes grandiosity; superiority entitles the bearer to special treatment and justifies taking advantage of others. Narcissists are often eaten up by envy of those who are more successful, and prone to fits of rage when they don't get their due, but they may otherwise get along quite well, particularly in business and politics. Their self-confidence and arrogance can be quite attractive to others, but their relationships are shallow, their personal lives can get messy, and all their success can't fill a hollowness within.

Personality disorders often come to light when a setback, a change in life circumstances, or simple aging makes it clear that things are awry—a person with narcissistic personality, for example, may have more than the usual difficulty negotiating the passage into middle age.

Or the pattern reveals itself when treatment for something more obvious, like anxiety or depression, runs into difficulty: the usual methods don't work, or while addressing the presenting problem, the process of therapy brings deeper issues to the surface. It has been estimated that as many as half of people seeking help for more acute psychiatric problems have personality disorders as well.

Effective treatment means reshaping the very basis of character; it's a long process. Psychodynamic therapy seems to work best, but certain forms of cognitive-behavioral therapy can be helpful, and pharmacotherapy may be indicated for specific symptoms of personality disorders.

## Adjustment Disorder

This term is used when symptoms of depression, anxiety, or disturbed behavior develop in response to a stressful event or situation. Adjustment disorder is the common cold of psychological problems.

It's only human to suffer when distressing or demanding things happen. You have trouble sleeping as things heat up at the office, cry frequently and can't concentrate after a marital breakup, become nervous and short-tempered when you're packing up the house to move. If your reaction goes beyond what seems reasonable to expect in the situation or significantly impairs your ability to work or get along with others, it becomes a "disorder."

Time and context are what distinguish an adjustment disorder from the conditions discussed above; it begins within three months (usually much sooner) of the stressful event or situation, and it lasts no longer than six months after the stress is over. It is only diagnosed in the absence of other psychological disorders (such as depression or generalized anxiety disorder).

Adjustment disorders are by definition self-limiting; when circumstances change, symptoms will resolve. But you may want to consider therapy to help you cope and minimize the damage (particularly if the stressor is chronic, such as a serious medical condition or challenging environment), and perhaps to strengthen your ability to deal with future crises. Behavioral approaches, particularly those that feature stress reduction, are an obvious choice, but brief psychodynamic or humanistic therapy can be helpful as well.

# References

American Psychiatric Association. AMA Principles of Medical Ethics with Annotations Especially Applicable to Psychiatry. [www.psych.org/apa_members/medicalethics2001_42001.cfm]

——. "Confidentiality." Fact sheet. 1998.

——. *Diagnostic and Statistical Manual of Mental Disorders.* 4th ed. Washington, D.C.: American Psychiatric Association, 1994.

——. "Managed Care and Your Mental Health." [www.psych.org/public_info/mancare.cfm]

——. "Memories of Sexual Abuse." Public Statement. 1993.

——. "Mental Health Bill of Rights Project: A Joint Initiative of Mental Health Professional Organizations." [www.psych.org/public_info/bill_rights.cfm]

——. *Practice Guideline for the Treatment of Major Depressive Disorder.* 2d ed. Washington, D.C.: American Psychiatric Press, 2000.

——. *Practice Guideline for the Treatment of Patients with Eating Disorders.* 2d ed. Washington, D.C.: American Psychiatric Press, 2000.

——. *Practice Guideline for the Treatment of Patients with Panic Disorder.* Washington, D.C.: American Psychiatric Press, 1998.

American Psychological Association. *Ethical Principles of Psychologists and Code of Conduct.* 1992.

——. "A Guide to Beneficial Psychotherapy." [www.apa.org/divisions/div12/rev_est/index.shtml]

——. *Talk to Someone Who Can Help.* Informational brochure, n.d.

Bateman, A., and P. Fonagy. "Treatment of Borderline Personality Disorder with Psychoanalytically Oriented Partial Hospitalization: An 18–Month Follow-up." *American Journal of Psychiatry* 158 (2001): 36–42.

Bozarth, J. *Person-Centered Therapy: A Revolutionary Paradigm.* Ross–on–Wye, U.K.: PCCS Books, 1998.

Chambless, D. L., and T. H. Ollendick. "Empirically Supported Psychological Interventions: Controversies and Practice." *Annual Review of Psychology* 52 (2001): 685–716.

*Clinical Psychiatry News* 15, no. 4 (April 1987).

Corsini, R., ed. *Handbook of Innovative Therapy.* 2nd ed. New York: Wiley, 2001.

Department of Consumer Affairs, State of California. "Professional Therapy Never Includes Sex." Consumer brochure, n.d.

"Do Informed Consent Letters Have a Role in Psychotherapy?" Forum, *Harvard Mental Health Letter* 15, no. 1 (1999): 9.

Edward, J. "Is Managed Mental Health Treatment Psychotherapy?" *Clinical Social Work Journal.* New York: Human Sciences Press, 1999.

Fehr, S. S. *Introduction to Group Therapy.* New York: Haworth Press, 1999.

Gay, P. *Freud: A Life for Our Time.* New York: Norton, 1988.

Glick, I. D., et al. *Marital and Family Therapy.* 4th ed. Washington, D.C.: American Psychiatric Press, 2000.

Goldenberg, I., and R. Goldenberg. *Family Therapy: An Overview.* 4th ed. Pacific Grove, Calif.: Brooks/Cole Publishing, 1996.

Goode, E. "How Much Therapy Is Enough? It Depends." *New York Times,* 24 November 1998.

Gurman, A. S., and S. B. Messer, eds. *Essential Psychotherapies.* New York: Guilford, 1995.

Gutheil, T. G., and G. O. Gabbard. "The Concept of Boundaries in Clinical Practice: Theoretical and Risk–Management Dimensions." *American Journal of Psychiatry* 150 (1993): 188–96.

Hubble, M. A., B. L. Duncan, and S. D. Miller. *The Heart and Soul of Change: What Works in Therapy.* Washington, D.C.: American Psychological Association, 1999.

Hymowitz, C. "Patients Pay a Price for Privacy—The Skirt Scrutiny, Some Refuse to File Insurance Claims." *Wall Street Journal,* 22 January 1998.

Imperio, W. "Online Therapy Sparks Concern." *Clinical Psychiatry News* 28, no. 11 (2000): 1.

International Society for Interpersonal Psychotherapy. "Interpersonal Therapy: An Overview." [www.interpersonalpsychotherapy.org]

Kahn, E. "Carl Rogers, More Relevant Today than Freud." *Psychotherapy Bulletin* 33 (1998): 35–36.

Levenson, H. *Time-Limited Dynamic Psychotherapy.* New York: Basic Books, 1995.

Luborsky, L., et al. "The Researcher's Own Therapy Allegiances: A 'Wild Card' in Comparisons of Treatment Efficacy." *Clinical Psychology: Science and Practice* 6 (1999): 95–106.

——, et al. "The Therapist Matters: Comparison of Outcomes Across Twenty-two Therapists and Seven Patient Samples." *Clinical Psychology: Science and Practice* 4 (1997): 53–65.

——, et al. *Who Will Benefit from Psychotherapy? Predicting Therapeutic Outcomes.* New York: Basic Books, 1988.

Macready, N. "Eye Movement Therapy Soothes Trauma Victims." *Clinical Psychiatry News* 29, no. 1 (2001): 44.

"Mental Health: Does Therapy Help?" *Consumer Reports,* November 1995.

Milrod, B., et al. "Open Trial of Psychodynamic Psychotherapy for Panic Disorder: A Pilot Study." *American Journal of Psychiatry* 157 (2000): 1878–80.

National Alliance for the Mentally Ill. "Hay Group Study on Health Care Plan Design and Cost Trends—1988 through 1997." [www.nami.org/pressroom/keyfind.html]

National Association of Social Workers. *National Association of Social Workers Code of Ethics,* n.d.

National Coalition of Mental Health Professionals and Consumers. *Mental Health Consumer Protection Manual.* Commack, N.Y., n.d.

National Institute of Mental Health. "The Numbers Count: Mental Disorders in America." [www.nimh.nih.gov/publicat/numbers.cfm]

Nicholi, A. M. *The Harvard Guide to Psychiatry.* Cambridge: Harvard University Press, 1999.

Pinsof, W. M., and L. C. Wynne. "The Efficacy of Marital and Family Therapy: An Empirical Overview, Conclusions, and Recommendations." *Journal of Marital and Family Therapy* 21, no. 4 (1995): 585–613.

Pollock, E. "Patients Pay a Price for Privacy—in Buyer's Market, Fee Negotiations Are Delicate Dance." *Wall Street Journal,* 22 January 1998.

Posthuma, B. W. *Small Groups in Counseling and Therapy.* 3d ed. Boston: Allyn and Bacon, 1999.

Seligman, M. E. P. "The Effectiveness of Psychotherapy: The Consumer Reports Study." *American Psychologist* 50, no. 12 (December 1995): 965–74.

Sherman, C. " 'Silence of the Lambs' Held Devastating to Psychiatry's Image." *Clinical Psychiatry News* 19, no. 5 (1991): 26.

Shorter, E. *History of Psychiatry.* New York: Wiley, 1997.

Silberschatz, G., and J. B. Persons. "How Useful for Psychotherapists Are Randomized Controlled Experiments?" *Harvard Mental Health Letter* 16, no. 1 (1999): 1.

Simon, R. I. "Boundaries in Psychotherapy: A Safe Place to Heal." *Harvard Mental Health Letter* 13, no. 12 (1997): 4–5.

Tasman, A., M. Riba, and K. Silk. *The Doctor-Patient Relationship in Pharmacotherapy.* New York: Guilford Press, 2000.

U.S. Department of Health and Human Services. *Mental Health: A Report of the Surgeon General.* Washington, D.C.: U.S. Department of Health and Human Services, 2000.

——. "Protecting the Privacy of Patients' Health Information: Summary of the Final Regulation." Fact sheet. 2000.

Wachtel, P. L. "Psychotherapy in the Twenty–first Century." *American Journal of Psychotherapy* 54, no. 4 (2000): 441–50.

Weisgerber, K. *The Traumatic Bond Between the Psychotherapist and Managed Care.* Northvale, N.J.: Jason Aronson, 1999.

Weissman, M., J. Markowitz, and G. Klerman. *Comprehensive Guide to Interpersonal Psychotherapy.* New York: Basic Books, 2000.

Yontef, G. *Awareness, Dialogue, and Process.* Highland, N.Y.: Gestalt Journal Press, 1993.

# Website Resources Directory

If you're doing your own Internet research, remember that sources vary enormously in quality. There's no foolproof way to tell the difference between websites stocked with valuable facts and those full of dangerous fallacies, but a few guidelines can help you assess reliability and accuracy.

- Who runs the page? What gives them credibility? Educational institutions, government agencies, and organizations (ending with *.org, .gov,* or *.edu*) are in general more reliable than commercial sponsors (although some commercial sites are excellent). Contact information for the site's sponsors should be posted at the bottom of the home page; click "About This Site" to find out more.
- Where does site content come from? Authors of articles and their qualifications should be indicated and sources of facts identified. Claims (about treatment effectiveness, for example) should be backed by evidence. Typos, misspellings, and grammatical errors suggest poor quality control.

Many sites carry seals to show certification by web-monitoring organizations: some are meaningful, some are not. One worthy of respect is the Health On the Net Foundation [www.hon.ch]. To carry its seal, a site must agree to a code of principles to promote accuracy and reliability. Click on the HON seal itself to make sure the site is a current member, review the HON code, and find more resources for assessing websites.

The Academy of Cognitive Therapy
http://academyofct.org/Links/CertifiedMembers.asp
American Association for Marriage and Family Therapy
www.aamft.org

American Counseling Association
www.counseling.org

American Group Psychotherapy Association
www.agpa.org

American Psychiatric Association
www.psych.org

American Psychoanalytic Association
http://apsa.org

American Psychoanalytic Foundation
www.cyberpsych.org/apf/links.html

American Psychological Association
www.apa.org

Anxiety Disorders Association of America
www.adaa.org

Association for Advancement of Behavior Therapy
http://www.aabt.org/CLINICAL/CLINICAL.htm

BehaveNet Inc
www.behavenet.com

Dr. Ivan's Depression Central
www.psycom.net/depression.central.html

EMDR Institute
www.emdr.com

Gestalt Therapy Page
www.gestalt.org

Health Systems Solutions
www.healthtechsys.com

HelpHorizons.com
www.helphorizons.com

International Network on Personal Meaning
www.meaning.twu.ca

International Society for Interpersonal Psychotherapy
www.interpersonalpsychotherapy.org

International Society for Mental Health Online
www.ismho.org

Internet Mental Health
www.mentalhealth.com

National Coalition of Mental Health Professionals and Consumers
www.nomanagedcare.org

National Commission on Quality Assurance
www.ncqa.org

National Institute of Mental Health
   www.nimh.nih.gov
National Mental Health Association
   www.nmha.org
*National Register of Health Service Providers in Psychology*
   www.nationalregister.com
Obsessive-Compulsive Foundation
   www.ocfoundation.org
Person-Centered International
   http://www.personcentered.com
Psyche Matters
   www.psychematters.com/psainst.htm
Psychwatch.com
   www.psychwatch.com/license.htm
Rational Emotive Behavior Psychotherapists referral list
      (Albert Ellis Institute members)
   http://www.rebt.org/refer.html
Solution-Focused Therapy web page
   www.enabling.org
TherapistLocator.net
   http://therapistlocator.net
videoShrink.com
   www.videoshrink.com

# Acknowledgments

A journalist is only as good as his sources, and I was exceptionally fortunate in mine. If there is insight or wise counsel in this book, credit must go to the psychologists and psychiatrists, social workers and scientists who so generously and articulately shared their intelligence and compassion. In particular: Judith Beck, Phoebe Prosky, Sharon Hymer, James McMahon, Ted Grossbart, Leon Hoffman, Lester Luborsky, Robert Leahy, James Pretzer, Jeffrey Binder, Jerold Bozarth, Karen Shore, David Hawkins, Harold Bernard, Frank Dattilio, Fred Piercy, Barbara Milrod, John Markowitz, and Allan Tasman. The words and ideas that are occasionally attributed to them in the text represent but a small part of their contribution.

Limitless thanks also to Judy Sternlight, a terrific editor and an even better friend, without whom this book quite literally never would have happened.

Understanding grows from experience, and I would have understood nothing about the vast subject of psychotherapy without the accumulated wisdom of countless experts whose books I read and whose talks I covered at scientific and clinical meetings, and whom I interviewed over the last twenty years. Or without the editors, especially those at *Clinical Psychiatry News*, who gave me the opportunity to work, and by working learn.

Finally, I am indebted to my friends for their support, encouragement, and good humor while I toiled, sometimes grumpily, on these pages. Most especially and with love, to Debbie.

# *Index*

## About the Author

CARL SHERMAN is a freelance journalist who has written about mental health and psychotherapy for many national publications, including *Psychology Today, Family Circle, Self, McCall's, Us, GQ,* and *Investor's Business Daily.* He is a columnist and contributing writer for *Clinical Psychiatry News,* and the author of three other books. He lives in New York City.

## About AtRandom.com Books

AtRandom.com Books, a new imprint within the Random House Trade Group, is dedicated to publishing original books that harness the power of new technologies. Each title, commissioned expressly for this publishing program, will be offered simultaneously in various digital formats and as a trade paperback.

AtRandom.com books are designed to provide people with choices about their reading experience and the information they can obtain. They are aimed at communities of highly motivated readers who want immediate access to substantive and artful writing on the various subjects that fascinate them.

Our list features expert writing on health, business, technology, culture, entertainment, law, finance, and a variety of other topics. Whether written in a spirit of play, rigorous critique, or practical instruction, these books possess a vitality that new ways of publishing can aptly serve.

For information about AtRandom.com Books and to sign up for our e-newsletters, visit www.atrandom.com.